DEDICATION

To our friends in the West who have provided us with wonderful insight and long flights, and to our students/clients who have taught us far more than we have taught them.

The Drone Pilot's Guide to Real Estate Operations

Douglas Spotted Eagle
Jennifer Pidgen

Who Is This Book Written For?

First and foremost, thank you for purchasing this book, likely in pursuit of greater learning and better practices in the field of UAS technology and opportunity. Without readers like yourself, this book would be without meaning.

We authored this book for readers who are already UAS pilots looking to broaden their horizons, for would-be UAS pilots who perhaps are working towards their FAA certification, and for real estate agencies considering hiring pilots for purposes of home inspection, marketing content development, or archival of real estate properties.

The primary goal is to document the subject from beginning to end including meeting with clients, bidding the job, planning the flight, understanding the ramifications of safety planning, environmental awareness, risk management, situational awareness, looking for the best angles and flight techniques, and post-production output (whew, that was a long paragraph, but understand we're looking to leave no stone unturned).

The techniques are presented in the form of ingredients that may be used as individual components or blended together as "recipes."

Although the framework of the contained material focuses on going beyond the basics, we've attempted to present advanced techniques of flight without being overly technical. Throughout the book, the "recipes" generally assume that the reader already has the necessary background to understand the topic at hand (e.g., general knowledge of UAV/sUAS/UAS (drones), photography/video, editing, basic risk management awareness, and the ability to communicate and comprehend real estate needs. etc.). Moreover, the "recipes" are often just skeletons that aim to provide essential information for getting started, but which require the reader to spend time flying to understand the details. As such, it is assumed that the reader knows to practice these applications to properly implement them into a workflow.

This document also assumes some basic business knowledge. There is an assumption of basic ability to keep records, log flights, understand the responsibilities of running a business, marketing, and executing a business plan.

This publication is also intended as a collection of "best practices" for pilots getting into real estate. There are certainly things "to-do" and things that one should not do in the chase of excellent imagery.

It is important for any real estate agent reading this book understand that a strong understanding of real estate does not a good pilot make. Each component is a separate step. Great UAS pilots may not be great photographers, let alone being a great photographer of real estate.

The same goes for real estate photographers. Skills in photographing real estate and a strong understanding of real estate does not a great pilot make. Treat each component with equal respect.

Learn to fly.

Learn to be a good photographer.

Then learn to photograph/shoot video of real estate.

Attempting to do any two simultaneously is a well-known recipe for disaster, and may be dangerous to person, property or animals.

This document isn't a book of "start a drone business in two weeks and be making loads of money." If that's what you're looking for, the internet has plenty of those sorts of websites, and while they're fun to check out, they're not very realistic.

Please recognize that UAS are not toys.

We purposefully have avoided the term "drone" throughout this book not to deny that these tools are often/frequently referred to as "drones," but rather to underscore the separation between "toy drones" and "useful tools." These tools in the real estate or "commercial environment" have the power to do damage and as a result, risk mitigation and safety play a large role in this publication.

We highly recommend practical training, allowing a third entity to observe and assess the flying skills of the reader. Frequently, we don't know what we don't know, and third-parties can provide observation, recommendations, and validation, frequently providing certifications and recognition of effort and skill. These recommendations, certifications, and recognitions may help build awareness of your organization and the efforts taken to achieve skills.

The framework of legal operations may be changing and will likely remain fluid for a few years to come. This does not offer opportunity however, to fly outside the rules or fly "under the radar." As a community of trailblazers, creating the path to accepted use of UAS in the National AirSpace (NAS), we have a responsibility to our community of pilots and the communities in which we live. Please obey the requirements of flight in your regional areas. Apply for waivers, demonstrate ability, and abide by the structure set forth in the Federal Aviation Regulations, also known as the "FARs."

Once again, we thank you for purchasing this publication; we're very proud of the series and the focus on specific uses for the UAS in various aspects of commercial/enterprise environments. Please let us know about your reading experience after completing the book; we're always in search of improvement and excellence.

Hoo'zoo n'aan' taa (Fly in beauty),

Douglas Spotted Eagle   Jennifer Pidgen

TABLE OF CONTENTS

UNDERSTANDING REGULATIONS & REQUIREMENTS

Using a drone for Real Estate image capture, film, modeling, or any other purpose falls under regulations for Commercial UAS requirements. *It is not possible to operate a UAV for real estate under hobbyist rules.*

The FAA definition of Commercial Use includes:

- Selling photos or videos taken from a UAS
- Using UAS to provide contract services, such as industrial equipment or factory inspection
- Using UAS to provide professional services, such as security or telecommunications
- Using UAS to monitor the progress of work your company is performing
- Professional real estate or wedding photography
- Professional cinema photography for a film or television production
- Providing contract services for mapping or land surveys

The ability to fly a UAS for commercial purposes is authorized via the FAA, through what many refer to as "Part 107." Part 107 is a section in the Federal Aviation Regulations (FARs) that regulates UAS flight. Part 107 is not the only portion of the FARs regulating UAS flight; there are other relevant FARs such as Part 91 (general operating and flight rules, covering weather conditions, reckless operation, drugs/alcohol).

A UAS Pilot candidate must be familiar with regulations found in Part 107, airspace regulation, ability to read a vector chart, knowledge of METARs and TAFs, weights/balances of aircraft, and best practices for safe, compliant UAS operations. Although the FAA 107 examination does not address State/Local regulations, an RPIC must become familiar with any local regulations as well.

WHAT IS REQUIRED TO OBTAIN A REMOTE PILOT CERTIFICATION?

Remote Pilot requirements:

- Must be at least 16 years of age
- Be able to read, speak, write, and understand English (exceptions may be made if the person is unable to meet one of these requirements for a medical reason, such as hearing impairment)
- Be in a physical and mental condition to safely operate a small UAS
- Pass the initial aeronautical knowledge exam at an FAA-approved knowledge testing center

UAS requirements:

- Must weigh less than 55 lbs.*
- Must undergo pre-flight check by remote pilot in command (a.k.a. you or the person supervising the operation)

Location requirements (click here for more details on these airspace classes):

- Operations in Class B, C, D and E airspace are allowed with the required Air Traffic Controller (ATC) permission

- Operations in Class G airspace are allowed *without* ATC permission

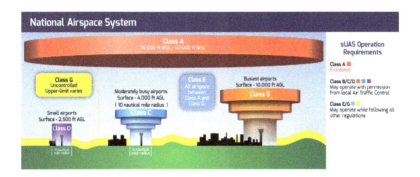

STATE/LOCAL ORDINANCES/LAWS

Although the FAA controls all aspects of the National Airspace (NAS), state law and county/city/town ordinances (municipalities) may control the grounds within the boundaries of their municipality. For example, an HOA cannot control the air above homes inside the HOA, yet the HOA may pass an ordinance that states that UAS may not be launched nor landed inside the confines of the HOA.

Many cities have ordinances about flying in neighborhoods or subdivisions; it is important to know local ordinances to avoid trouble. Do an online search or contact the local police department for information on local ordinances. UAS laws are still very fluid and very new; it is recommended to verify sources whenever possible.

Ordinance No. 330-16

**Council Members Zone, Keane and Kelley
(by departmental request)**

AN EMERGENCY ORDINANCE
To supplement the Codified Ordinances of
Cleveland, Ohio, 1976, by enacting new Section
490.01, 490.02, 490.03, and 490.99, relating to
unmanned aircraft systems.

WHEREAS, the operation of unmanned aircraft systems ("UAS") has recently

increased significantly both locally and nationally and numerous incidents have occurred

involving UAS operations in restricted areas without compliance with existing Federal

Aviation Administration ("FAA") regulatory guidance; and

WHEREAS, there is currently no legislation that regulates UAS in the City

of Cleveland or provides specific enforcement authority to safety forces

WHEREAS, this situation poses a significant enforcement

officers; and

WHEREAS, the United States Government

the United States under 49 U.S.C. § 40103

WHEREAS, the FAA has issued

Unauthorized UAS Operations

best position to deter, discover, and

stop unauthorized UAS

WHEREAS

usual daily

FEDERAL REGULATIONS

Once a Remote Pilot Certification (RPC) is received, the certificate does not simply mean the aircraft can be flown anywhere, so long as the 400' regulation is observed. For example, flying within Class B, C, or D airspace requires permission from the FAA regardless of the RPC. Flying over non-involved persons, flying at night, flying beyond the visual line of sight (VLOS) are not permitted without specific permission known as a "waiver."

If a potential home is within controlled airspace, a waiver is required. Waivers may be applied for on-line at https://faadronezone.faa.gov/#/

It is our recommendation that regardless of need for a waiver, apply for any waivers that may be needed in the future. Apply to gain practice and fluency in "FAA-Speak." Expect initial applications to be denied.

In filing waivers, never copy waivers found online; the application will be immediately denied. Consider all components of the waiver, write requests in language that mirrors language used in the FAR or FSIMs for best results.

Once Certificates of Waiver (COWs) or Certificate of Authorization (COA) are received, make multiple paper copies. One copy should be a component in the Policy/Procedures/Operations manual while another copy is kept on-site during all operations. While a digital copy is permissible, it is not advised in the event of loss of WiFi, depleted battery on a phone or tablet, etc.

It is possible to fly without motors, but not without knowledge and skill.

— Wilbur Wright

INSURANCE

As with any business venture, insurance is not legally required, yet no prudent business person would consider operating without insurance *(Insurance is required if operating in some foreign countries. Canada as one example, requires insurance for commercial operations).*

In aviation, there are two primary forms of insurance; *Liability and Hull.*

Hull Insurance

Hull insurance insures the aircraft itself and is relatively inexpensive. When purchasing hull insurance, consider the cost of the insurance over the period of 12 months and evaluate the return on investment (ROI). For example, insuring the hull of a small UAS may cost $500 per year, while the replacement cost of the aircraft is $800. This many or may not be an appropriate ROI.

Liability Insurance

Liability insurance is the insurance that is there as protection in the event of an incident that may be expensive. For example, while flying, the UAS strikes a phone or powerline, damaging the cable.

Aside from any induced fines, this sort of incident has already seen precedent at a personal cost to a pilot of over $100,000. Liability insurance would generally cover this sort of incident (assuming all regulations are being met at the time of inci-dent). Ask the insurer if the policy covers Personal Injury, Invasion of Privacy Claims, Damage to Public or Private Prop-erty, and Medical Expenses.

Depending on the agency, liability insurance carries a cost between $600-$1000 per year for a recommended minimum of $1M. This cost can be reduced through participation in augmented/recurrent training programs, ISO audit, type of work, and time-in-industry.

Liability insurance also protects the business owner/pilot from liability costs in the event of an injury. UAS have sharp blades spinning at high speeds, and injuries do occur from time to time. It is recommended that a minimum policy of $1M in liability insurance is in place to protect the business.

It is rare that homeowner, business owner, or apartment ten-ant insurance will cover aviation activity of any kind. Check with the insurance carrier to ensure that the policy specifi-cally covers UAS or aviation activity.

Business Acumen

There are no secrets to success. It is the result of preparation, hard work, and learning from failure.

— Colin Powell

The commercial drone (UAV/sUAS) industry is exploding as a variety of organizations look to implement this new technology into their business workflows. The key to a successful small Unmanned Aerial System (sUAS) implementation is in the planning and understanding how this technology fits into a real estate business strategy. Throughout this handbook, one message should shine through: *Planning is key to success.* Planning implementation, planning interactions with customers, planning communications with third parties, and ultimately, planning UAV flights.

Crawl. Walk. Run. It is a common model applied within many spheres of life and it is well practiced as a successful business discipline. With the excitement of UAVs (Unmanned Aerial Vehicles) as a new technology, it's easy to be swept up in the frenzy. It's critical when implementing sUAS as an aerial tool with a company's toolbox to take the time to plan before running (or flying!) with the idea.

Crawl	• Be aware of the excitement/pressure to add sUAS as a tool • Define the high-level requirement of sUAS within the business • Outline financial benefits of sUAS applied within the business
Walk	• Research, research, research • Define and refine the business' policy procedures and operations (PPO) manual for sUAS • Test and train with aircraft and software that fit the business strategy

Run	• Selection of technology partner(s)
	  ○ Aircraft
	  ○ Software (image/video editing, aircraft & personnel management)
	• Refine PPO
	• Strategy refinement: Focus on differentiation from norm & profitability

Fly	• Officially Implement new sUAS program for the business (market & sell) • Add new flying techniques with gained flight experience • Add new editing stylings with gained experience • Integrate with ground footage, virtual tours, etc. • Update organizations PPO

REAL ESTATE BUSINESS STRATEGY

The distinction between success and failure boils down to six words. The successful ones "Think Big, Start Small, Learn Fast.
— Chunka Mui

The importance of having a business strategy cannot be understated; strategy sets the direction of every business. Strategy is the result of choices made; the better the choices, the better the strategy. Strategy and choices are as much about what to do as what not to do. Business strategy is built as choices are executed; strategy is about transformation and acting on choices. This section will focus on how to position sUAS into the real estate business model, how to increase the value of services provided, and decrease the risk involved (or perceived) in flying a UAV over homes.

As a sUAS field service provider (FSP), the first question is: "What do I need to know about real estate to provide competitive services to real estate agents or agencies."

As a real estate agent, the first question, in terms of strategic implementation should be: *"Do I want to become a certified remote pilot* **OR** *do I want to hire a remote pilot as a service to supplement my service offerings."* Either application of sUAS as a tool is valid, but the implementation process differs.

The following sections will focus on these three methods of sUAS implementation, offer insights on what to expect, and will specify what is needed for a successful integration into the business' workflow.

Remote Pilots looking to offer sUAS Services to Real Estate Agents & Agencies

> *Strive not to be a success, but rather to be of value.*
> — Albert Einstein

As a 107 certificated pilot and sUAS field service provider looking to increase streams of revenue, an obvious choice would be to offer video and photography services to real estate professionals. The learning curve for real estate services is understanding what the client will require as an end product from flights in the field (photography vs. video), how to quote on services provided (field time and/or editing time), ensuring safety and consistency if the FSP company has several pilots, and onsite prep for sUAS flights.

Crawl: Understanding Real Estate

Before creating a list of sUAS services for real estate, it's imperative to understand the verticals within real estate. Take time to research the local real estate market as every area is unique and its service needs will necessarily be unique as well. For example, affluential areas will likely require more aerial photos and video than other areas.

> **Four Categories of Real Estate:**
>
> (1) Residential   (2) Commercial
>
> (3) Industrial   (4) Land

There are four primary categories of real estate:

Residential Real Estate

This is the most common vertical in real estate. It includes both resale homes and new construction homes. sUAS services would be applicable for single-family homes, condominiums, co-ops, duplexes, and quadplexes, townhouses, triple-deckers, luxury homes, and vacation homes.

Commercial Real Estate

This real estate vertical focuses on buildings (and areas) which are owned to produce income. sUAS services would be focused on shopping centers and strip malls, hotels, offices, (medical, legal), educational buildings, and often apartment and condo buildings which are owned by property management companies.

Industrial Real Estate

sUAS services for this real estate vertical would focus on warehouses (storage and distribution centers), research facilities, factories and manufacturing buildings and property. The

Image Courtesy of Maurice King

differentiation between Industrial and Commercial real estate is based on its *zoning*. This classification is important as construction and sales are handled differently for industrial real estate.

Land

This real estate vertical includes vacant land (undeveloped, early development or reuse areas), working farms and ranches, subdivision or wholesaling areas and  a highly niched area of site location and parcel assembly. Each of these subcategories require specialized real estate knowledge.

Once decided on which of the verticals to focus on, it's easier to set a direction for sUAS services to be provided. The process of capturing images and video for each vertical will be the same but understanding the perspective and needs of the (client) will be unique for each. Starting with one vertical is recommended before folding in a second. For the purposes of easier reading, the manual will focus on sUAS flight for residential real estate. The points made, for the most part, transition into the other three verticals as well.

Walk: sUAS Services Offered & Policy Procedure and Operations Manuals

 The importance of a business Policy, Procedure, and Operations manual (PPO) cannot be underestimated. This manual becomes the foundation upon which the services provided can grow beyond the owner of the company. Its purpose is to ensure consistency of sUAS

flights, data capture for each project, expectations of staff (dress code, interactions, etc.), steps to incorporate safety in every flight/project, and risk management procedures when things go awry. The PPO is a living document. In other words, it is a document that *necessarily needs to be reviewed and updated on a regular basis.* It is recommended to have this living document review (at least) annually.

In a nutshell, the PPO provides a step-by-step system for day-to-day operations, with a focus on safety and risk management, compliance to health and safety, legal liabilities, and regulatory requirements, and management of issues that may have serious consequence to the organization. It's a playbook for streamlining internal processes and offers guidance for decision-making. (e.g. Is the job requested too risky? Are there safety concerns that can be mitigated? How would they be mitigated?) It also includes a detailed understanding of what equipment is being used, how the equipment is to be maintained, and the overall workflow of a typical sUAS project.

> **The Policy, Procedures, and Operations manual(s) are LIVING documents which need to be reviewed at least annually.**

The specifics of a PPO manual are outside the scope of this manual, but there are many templates available online as a good starting point. There are also qualified organizations offering their consulting services to assist in writing PPO manuals. A good starting point is to make sure the research has been thorough, and the game plan moving forward is clear. Solid research is a good foundation for any PPO. This manual will touch upon quite a few areas contained within a PPO for real estate. A high-level overview for a real estate structured PPO follows.

Test and Train with Aircraft and Software Solutions that Fit the Business Strategy

During the walking stage of building out the real estate service offerings for the business, it's important that there is flexibility in trying a variety of equipment options and software solutions. This step is about research, testing, and researching some more. Research equipment options, what are the pros/cons of each small unmanned aerial system (sUAS); what's their ease of use? Limitations? Expansion ability?

This manual goes into greater detail on the questions to be answered when looking to make an investment in a sUAS. This chapter focuses how to best select the right aircraft for your needs.

> Before investing in equipment, take the time to demo a variety of sUAS in the market.

While "walking", take the time to fly a variety of sUAS in the market. Join a meetup group, connect with a local retailer and have them demonstrate the options available. Join a Facebook group or LinkedIn group and get involved in conversations. Test a variety of software solutions that meet the business needs; many solutions offer a free 30-day trial before a commitment is required. Take advantage of the free trial periods and put it to work. Once the kinks have been worked out, it's time to finalize the business' PPO.

Policy, Procedure and Operation Manual for Real Estate

- Certification Cards of Pilots
  - Include all pilots flying for the organization
- Introduction to PPO Manual
  - This is the section detailing the "why" behind the document, the commitment to remaining compliant with the Federal Aviation Regulations (FARs), and the assurance that all personnel have read the PPO.
  - Where possible, list all personnel within the document and record when the PPO was last updated
- Safety Policy
  - This is an over-arching vision of how operations are to be managed by the organization; ultimately with the highest safety standards in mind. This includes:
    - Monitoring and measuring safety performance of personnel and systems
    - Continuous awareness of current safety practices within the aviation industry

- ❏ Encouragement of safety information collection, analysis and exchange amongst all relevant industry organizations
- ❏ Allocation of resources (financial and human) for safety management, training, and oversight
- Statement of Just Culture
- Best Practices Compliance Statement
  - ○ Focuses on ensuring appropriate safety standards, industry standardization and reflects global best practice in the conduct of Remotely Piloted Operations. It's a promise to keep abreast of industry changes as they happen and committing to keeping the living document amended to reflect changes.
- List of relevant business documents
  - ○ Real Estate Project Questionnaire
    - ❏ To create the statement of work and understand the scope of the project
  - ○ Safety Checklists
    - ❏ Pre-planning
    - ❏ On-Site Planning
    - ❏ Post-Flight Data maintenance
  - ○ Templates of Flight Announcements
    - ❏ Neighborhood announcements/flyers
    - ❏ HOA letters
    - ❏ Police letters
  - ○ Waivers (if necessary)
  - ○ Mutual NDA (if necessary)
- FAA Regulatory Guideline, Directions, Permissions and Approvals

- Overview of FAA guidelines and expectations
  - Definitions NOTAMs/DROTAMs requirements
- Alcohol, Drug, Fatigue and Health Management
- Privacy
- Occupational Health & Safety
  - Use of Personal Protective Equipment (safety vests, area signage, etc.)
  - Availability of First Aid kits
- Maintenance and Log Requirements
  - Pilot's Flight Logs
  - UAV Flight Logs & Maintenance
  - Battery Logs
- Operations Specific
  - Purpose
  - Persons Authorized
  - Area of Operations
  - Plan of Activities
    - Safety!

1. Introduction

A. Purpose

This manual has been developed by "Sundance Media Group, LLC", hereafter referred to as "SMG", in conjunction with an application for a Certificate of Waiver or Authorization of the provisions of FAR 91.119 (b) and (c) for the purpose of filming. SMG pilots and other company personnel when applicable will comply with the policies, procedures, and conditions of this manual, whenever motion picture or television flight operations are performed that require a Waiver of Authorization as mentioned above.

- Preflight standards
- Clearing the area
- Announcements (Power, launch, land)
- Weather maximums (aircraft-based)
- Risk mitigation practices (powerlines, antenna lines, TV antenna, other obstacles)
- Permission to Operate
  - Waiver requirements
  - Property owners
  - Law enforcement officials
  - Fire department officials
  - Local, State and Federal government
- Security
- Briefing of Pilot/Production Personnel
- Certification/Airworthiness
- Pilot Personnel/Minimum Requirements
- Communications
  - Interacting with Real Estate Agencies
    - What do they expect (if they could have anything...)?
    - Editing responsibility
  - Interaction with home owners
    - Prepping the homeowner for the flight
      - Staging outside of home, yard, automobiles, windows/doors etc.
      - Time required for flight/ensure home owner does not enter nor leave home during flight.

- ○ Interaction with neighbors
  - ❑ Forewarn with notices on doors
    - ✰ Notify them of flight areas
    - ✰ Ensure they understand what will be captured
    - ✰ Flight launch time/land time (duration)
- ○ Accident Notification
- ○ Recall/Stop Procedures
- ○ Aerobatic Competency
- ○ Duties and Responsibilities of Personnel
- ○ Specific UAV Flight Conduct
- ○ Importance of consistent flight & data capture
  - ❑ Data Management & File Naming
  - ❑ GPS Meta Data
- Document Revision Control Page

Run: Equipment Selection and Workflow Refinement

 Now that the business strategy is defined, the research completed (is it ever really complete?), and the PPO is written, it's time to RUN! This is where the business begins to solidify. It's time to make the investment in the chosen equipment, software programs (data collection, video editing, accounting, etc.), and refine the PPO accordingly. As jobs begin to materialize this is an ongoing learning and refinement process. Keep the focus on how the business strategy is differentiated from the competition and of course, keep track **profitability**. Cash flow, in this phase, is likely going to be negative flows, but it is all part of building the future of the service pipeline.

> **Be sure to keep track of the bottom line!**

Part of the process of running a self-owned field service provider (FSP) business is managing the bottom line. That can be tricky and often new business operators underestimate the amount of time/energy  a project might take. This section offers a few insights to what should be considered when bidding on projects.

Bidding on Project

Before accepting a project, it is key to **clearly understand what the client is looking for**. Is it raw images / video? Is it required to create a final produced product? What are the expectations for reshoots or re-edits.

> **Set up a Scope of Work document with the client to ensure clear communication of expectations for each project.**

Below are a few (surely not all!) points to keep in mind when bidding on a project:

- **What is the goal of the project?** What is the finished product requested?
  - Ask the client: "If you could have whatever you want, what would it look like?"
    - Think big, then scale accordingly

- Define the entire Scope of Work (SOW) with the client
  - Expected/Suggested Shot list
    - Aerial only? Or will there be a need for ground images/video as well?
    - Interiors? (while not related to flying for a gig, it may be a requirement for the project – does this fit within the defined business strategy?)
  - Detail what the prep time is (battery/aircraft management, site scouting, etc. See the chapter on pre-planning steps for more specific details and on-site prep details can be found here.
  - Detail overall flight time – this will help keep track of battery requirements and usage
  - Estimated Post-production time (if this is included in the project)
  - Discuss a plan of action and/or limitations to reshoots/re-edits

Timeline & Milestones

Timeline Overview	Milestone Deadline
SOW Release	May 19, 2017
Advertising Images & Video from PS Event May 11/12/13	May 21, 2017
Coordinate access of an HS20 for Sgt. Marvin and/or Prosser (NAAP)	
Coordinate access of CSO 1?	
Confirmation of NAAP & CAP	May 26, 2017
Coordinate logistics for the AR – UAS segment with NAAP & CAP	May 29, 2017
Location Inspection & Confirmation	June 2, 2017
Arrange for an HS20 testimonial from Sgt. Marvin and/or Prosser (NAAP)	June 9, 2017
Arrange for an HS20 testimonial from James Spear (LAP)	June 9, 2017
Arrange/coordinate AR – UAS for filming prior to event with NAAP & CAP	June 16, 2017
Coordinate logistics with NAAP & CAP for AR – UAS Presentation	June 16, 2017
Planning, coordination, and implementation of Attendee Fly Day	June
Coordinate Logistics onsite as needed during the event for TBD – of 3	
Coordinate logistics onsite as needed during the event for Fly Day	

- *Insurance* – will the business' current insurance offer enough coverage for this project? Will any additional costs be incurred by a need to increase coverage? (**See Chapter on Insurance for more info**)
- *Waiver Requirements* – Have necessary waivers already been obtained? Can one be rented from a pilot owning the waiver needed? Or, alternatively, is there time to wait for a waiver application to be filed?

Here are some of the documents that a potential client will be looking for from their FSPs:

- Portfolio of recently completed projects
- RPC document
- Copy of W-9
- Company License numbers
- Insurance agreements
- Dun & Bradstreet (big gigs)
- 3 Supplier References
- Lead Time Requirements
- Weather Conditions & Reshoot Policy
- Deposit, Cancellation & Rescheduling Policy
- Blank Contract for Services Hired

Determining the right price point for the project is not as easy as some might believe. It's an art form in itself, but fortunately there are a lot of online resources that can assist with this process and there are a variety of ways to price out a project. Below are some of the most common ways to price an FSP project.

Methods of Pricing: Custom Quotes, Hourly Pricing, Turnaround Time, Content Produced: Photos & Video

Custom Quoting each Project

Pros:

- Ability to offer a price range for services provided
- Great for unique or specialized projects
- Selling point: clients get exactly what they are paying for

Cons:

- Not easy to apply across jobs – still require basic set pricing for time spent on a project
- Clients may be concerned about value if pricing is not standardized

Hourly Pricing

Pros:

- Simple format, easy to apply to many projects
- If the project is shorter than estimated, bonus for FSP

Cons:

- Estimates may be off and for challenging projects with reshoots/reedits, FSP may find his/her hourly rate diminish

Turnaround Time

Pros:

- Offers the client budget options on less time-sensitive projects

Cons:

- Challenging to organize when juggling multiple projects

Content Produced: Photos (Can be combined with hourly pricing for flight)

Pros:

- Pricing focuses on specific output needs to the client (Image Size, Resolution, Editing / Retouching needs and quantity of Images)
- Ability to offer a variety of price-point packages to the client

Cons:

- Remote pilot must become a confident photo editor and understand the time required for managing images
- Additional training may be required

Content Produced: Video (Can be combined with hourly pricing for flight)

Pros:

- Pricing focuses on specific output needs to the client (Video length, music/graphic overlay, etc.)
- Ability to offer a variety of price-point packages to the client

Cons:

- Remote pilot must become a confident video editor and understand the time invested for cutting video together
- Additional training may be required

Do not be surprised if pricing a project becomes a moving target. The FSP industry is still in its founding stages and with the flood of new FSPs in the market, that "perfect formula" is elusive.

Be flexible. Be adaptable. But most importantly, **do not undersell the value of the service provided.** The business can only thrive once it goes beyond breaking even.

> For some projects, a mix-n-match of pricing schemes might be used. Be creative, but keep track of the bottom line.

FLY: Getting off the Ground & Flying Beyond the Basics

The business strategy and foundation are set; equipment and software workflow are functioning smoothly; the sUAS program is implemented and being actively marketed and sold. The next step is recognizing what is involved in having the business (pardon the pun) truly take off. While not an easy question to answer, there are a few tips and tricks that can be added into the business toolset to add to the business' differentiation in the market as well as increase the quality of services provided. Ultimately the key is three-fold: continue to do research, continue to learn, and market the services to local real estate agencies.

Continue to Learn as a Pilot and as a Content Producer

Working with images, no matter what the subject matter, can become dated. Add to that, working with a templated system (the easiest way to make sure shots are collected in the field is to check-off the shots is from a shot list) means there is little creativity in the mix. Real estate, no matter the specific category, is about marketing a property – to sell it, or rather, make it look enticing enough to buy. In other words, the content being created is **marketing** the property in question. Marketing necessarily needs to keep fresh, otherwise the message can be dull and be lost in amongst other messages. Following are some suggestions on ways to keep adding unique perspectives into the service provided, as a pilot and as a content producer.

1. Continue to try (and master) new flight techniques. See the chapter on additional shots to consider later in the manual.

   o Consider professional practical training workshops to learn how to master challenging techniques without all the trials and errors of "figuring it out on your own".

   o With gained flight experience pilots should endeavor to build upon their techniques; more complicated flight patterns and combinations can create more exciting content such as:

     i. **Precision Flying** – get closer to a key subject area

     ii. **Pass Thru Flying** – fly through two buildings before revealing the aerial view

2. For service providers creating videos and images for their clients, another key is to continue to add new editing stylings with gained experience (See the chapter on editing for examples)

- ○ e.g. Transitions / Titles / Bottom Thirds / Color Correction
- ○ There is a myriad of tutorials online to learn how to edit images and cut video together, including some on fun and interesting techniques.
- ○ Consider taking in-class workshops or attend a tradeshow offering a variety of educational sessions dedicated to increasing skills and efficiency with photo and video editing.

3. Go beyond the aerial content

- ○ Integrate the end product with ground footage and images

- ○ Include access to virtual tours, etc.

> **The importance of keeping the business service offerings current and unique is key to the business' differentiation and ultimately its success in a quickly growing market of FSPs.**

Continue to Research and Update PPO

As a new technology, sUAS as a tool is changing quickly. The aircrafts available, the cameras flown, the software being used to process the data, and, from a business per-

spective, the administrative software tools available (accounting software, fleet management, insurance offerings) change and evolve. It's important, as a business owner, time is taken to keep abreast of new offerings, shifts in technology, and possible savings. "Savings" can be found financially (think more inexpensive insurance offerings) or time saved (consider a more efficient software program cutting time out of the workflow). The key to this? Research. As an entrepreneur, the step of research is never really over.

As changes are made to the sUAS workflow, it is recommended to update the PPO accordingly. Any changes, or additions to the business workflow, or additions to the equipment list need to be updated in the organization's PPO. Ideally as changes occur, the PPO should be updated. Realistically, schedule an annual PPO review to ensure updates are managed. If time and resources allow, the PPO should be reviewed bi-annually, especially in such a fast-moving industry as sUAS.

> **REMINDER: A PPO is a living document; it needs to be updated when changes within the organization occur.**

Marketing Real Estate sUAS Services

As a field service provider (FSP) offering a new service within a new industry (in this case real estate), it's vital to the businesses success to market-

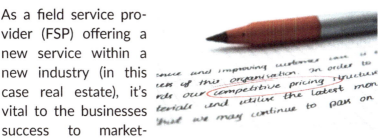

ing its services. Reach out to local real estate agencies; join social media groups dedicated to the industry; create flyers to hand out at local events, or even real estate open houses (a great way to meet local real estate agencies!). Marketing doesn't need to be an expensive adventure, often grassroots or guerilla methods work best. The concept is to find inexpensive ways to introduce the new real estate sUAS services to local agencies, agents, and potential venders. The power of shaking hands and offering an informational flyer should not be underestimated. As in any business, relationship building is key.

REAL ESTATE AGENTS AND AGENCIES LOOKING TO ADD sUAS AS A SERVICE

Great things in business are never done by one person. They're done by a team of people.

— Steve Jobs

There is little debate regarding the benefit of differentiating property listings through high-quality photography and video. As a real estate agent, coming from within the real estate industry, the business issues of adding aerial photos and video to the sales and marketing workflow is focused on the "how" to add this as an option to for clients. There are two ways agents and agencies can embrace this new aerial vison of properties. Contracting out the service to a Field Service Provider (FSP) or building out an sUAS program internally. There are pros and cons to either choice; the biggest deciding factor should be: Is there someone within the business who will be committed to researching, learning, implementing, and applying this new technology for the organization. If yes, then skip over this section to read how to implement an sUAS program within the real estate business.

This section will focus on the steps of **contracting out** sUAS services to a Field Service Provider (FSP).

Here's a quick summary of the PROs & CONs of contracting out sUAS services:

PROs	CONs
• Speed of Implementation	• Time required to interview & consider FSP qualifications
• No need for investment of:	• Ability to find the right "fit" from an FSP
○ UAV Equipment & Accessories	• Lack of control of a project
○ sUAS Software programs (i.e. fleet management)	• Flexibility - ability to "move quickly" on last minute projects (even if a qualified FSP is known, he/she may not be available when required for last minute projects)
○ Editing Software programs	
• No requirement to keep up to date on FAA regulations, certification requirements, and airspace requirements	• Quality Control - many FSP are pilots first and editors second (quality of videos/images provided)
• No additional insurance requirements	• Safety/Risk Mitigation (need to understand remote pilot's PPO)
• Ability to hire several FSPs for variety in output and/or specialty projects	

Crawl: Define the Aerial need for the Real Estate Business

Before seeking out an sUAS Field Service Provider (FSP), it's important to define the need for aerial images and video within the agency. The specific need is dependent upon the focus of real estate vertical (aerial content (and other images) for a luxury home will be different than aerial content for an industrial building). That said, but for the most part, it is similar across the categories of real estate. The point here is to put some thought and planning behind what the ultimate goal is to offer aerial content into the real estate sales and marketing mix. By taking the time to define the shot

list for the client, the request for quote (RFQ) to the field service provider almost writes itself. Within the Planning Chapter, the manual goes into detail with a typical shot list for real estate. Here the focus is key differentiations for each category of real estate.

> **Define the need for aerial images and video within the real estate agency before seeking a FSP.**

Residential Real Estate

- Aerials of neighborhood (e.g. nearby parks and schools)
- Aerials leading into the property
- Unique angles of interesting areas of the property (e.g. pool, landscaping, etc.) ⑧ create a sense of awe
- If possible - aerials of local township/town/city

Commercial Real Estate

- Aerials of neighborhood
- Aerials leading into the property
- Aerials including various times of day (often twilight shots of commercial properties can be a stunning add to the selling portfolio)
- Inspection aerials

Industrial Real Estate

- Aerials of entire industrial area
- Local building panorama
- Aerials of specific areas of interest (smoke stacks, towers, etc.)

Land

Aerial requirements for undeveloped land is straight-forward. That said, if time allows, consider adding:

- Seasonal aerials
- Aerials from various times of day (Sunrise, mid-day, and sunset)

Define the Financial Benefits of Adding sUAS Services to the Business

To offer this new service to clients, a bit of research is required to determine what local FSPs are charging **and** what clients would actually pay for the service. As with any business decision, it's paramount to realize some return on investment. In this case, the investment is time spent sourcing  an FSP and offering the service. For example, if the local FSP is charging $500 for the service, it's important to know whether or not the market served by the business will support that added fee. If you skipped over the section for Remote Pilots looking to offer services to real estate agents/agencies, take the time to see the section on pricing bidding on a job. This is a good overview of how a FSP will quote his or her services.

Walk: Finding a FSP, the RFQ Process and Project Expectations

 With an understanding of what sUAS services are needed for clients, it's time to send the request for quote (RFQ) out to area FSPs. This process should be as templated as possible to make it easier when repeating the process for future projects. Include this new process/template within the organization's Policy, Procedure, and Operations (PPO) manual.

> **Template the RFQ process for ease of replication for future projects.**

Where to Find Field Service Providers (FSPs)

There are many ways to find local commercial remote pilots. A quick google search for "how to find a drone pilot" should bring up a few service providers who amalgamate pilot information and offerings. At the time of  writing this manual, Droners.io, AirVid.com and Skytango.com are three websites that will offer this service. Other ways to find a local FSP is to reach out to local MeetUp groups, post a request for a remote pilot on LinkedIn or on Facebook groups focused on commercial operations.

What to look for in a Remote Pilot FSP for Real Estate

This is highly dependent upon what the project entails, but the basics are:

- RPC Certification Document (better known as the Part 107 certification)
- Company License numbers & Proof of Insurance
- Portfolio of Recently Completed Projects (do their projects look/feel similar to what is required?)
  - ○ Interior Video and/or ground-based video abilities
- Pre-Shoot Planning Checklist (See Chapter on Planning for more info)
- Copy of W-9
- Dun & Bradstreet Rating for big gigs
- 3 Supplier References
- Lead Time & Weather Conditions
- Deposit, Cancellation & Rescheduling Policy

Submit Request for Quote (RFQ)

In the beginning, before having a qualified pilot on-call for the business, it might take a few trials to find the right pilot and service to fit the ongoing sUAS real estate services required. A common business practice to start this "weeding" process, is to send out an RFQ to three (3) FSPs for every project requiring aerial services. This will help to:

- Allow the agency an opportunity to experience different pilots
- Ensure a more "fair" service fee for the project quoted
- Refine the RFQ process for the organization (be sure to update the PPO manual!)

> **Best Practices for RFQ process: find three (3) FSPs who will bid on the quote.**

Project Expectations & RFQ Template

It is imperative that the RFQ submitted is clear and concise. It must detail specifics required for the project, milestones for completion (both dates and product) and payment terms. The more information contained within the RFQ, the better equipped the FSP will be to offer a fair quote on services provided. Following are some key points to be included with every RFQ.

1. Invitation to Quote
   o Request for qualifications (see previous section for specifics)
   o Executive Summary of the Project
   o RFQ Process, including release date (when the RFQ was published) and due date (when the FSP is required to reply by)

2. Project Coordination and Administration
   - ○ Name & Contact of Project Manager
   - ○ How questions from the FSP will be managed (phone or email or both?)
3. Detailed Overview of Project
   - ○ Project background and description
   - ○ Scope of work (be as specific as possible)
   - ○ Requested services and deliverables (including deliverables and milestones)
4. Submittal Requirements and Evaluation Criteria
   - ○ Qualifications of the FSP (Is there a specific expertise required? Insurance requirements?)
   - ○ Is there a specific method of pricing preferred (See section on "Bidding on the Project" for more)?
5. Selection Process & Schedule
   - ○ Submission requirements (how many copies of the proposal? Digital submission allowed or in-print only?)
   - ○ How will FSPs be compared to one another?
   - ○ Interviews required?
   - ○ Number of references called?

Run: Final Products from the FSP

With the new aerial service offering defined and the RFQ process completed (and drone FSP selected, it's time to RUN! It is time to ensure the quality of the deliverable before sharing it with the end-client. If the image (or video) quality does not meet the real estate agency's standards, don't be afraid to ask for reshoots, reedits, or even the raw data to manage the content internally if necessary. Again, finding the right remote pilot (and editor) may take a few tries. It is important to be honest with the chosen FSP and insist on a high-quality end product. Be sure the deliverable matches the original vision.

This "final product process" will shift and evolve over the first few projects. Be sure to refine the RFQ template as these needs come to light. Remember to also update the PPO manual accordingly. As projects pass through the real estate agency, this ongoing learning and refinement process will keep this new service aligned with the core business strategy and ulti-mately prepare the best sales and marketing assets for clients.

FLY: Bringing it all Together

After completing a few successful projects, it's time to consider a couple of business decisions for ease of future planning.

- Has the agency sourced one or two drone FSPs that can be contracted annually?
  - Eliminates the need to send the projects out for quote
- Find ways to consult directly with the drone FSP to build out new and exciting real estate sales and marketing tools
  - Extended videos including neighborhoods, or local points of interest
  - Include an option for virtual reality tours
- Offer Clients Additional Services (new revenue stream)
  - Property Appraisals
  - Home Inspections (for buyers interested in a home)
  - Insurance Documentation (After a property damage event such as flood, fire, theft)
  - Monitoring Land Erosion or Turf Maintenance Needs (Golf Courses or Park Services)
  - Documenting Property Lines **OR**
  - Renovation Planning

As business experience is developed with this new service offering, the sky is no longer the limit. Offering dramatic aerial images of a real estate property is truly the next evolution in real estate marketing and it will offer a point of differentiation in a particularly brutal and competitive market.

REAL ESTATE AGENTS AND AGENCIES LOOKING TO IMPLEMENT A sUAS PROGRAM

> *Every once in a while, a new technology, an old problem, and a big idea turn into an innovation.*
>
> — *Dean Kamen*

There is no doubt there is excitement within the real estate industry for sUAS as a tool; it has already been quite impactful! The ability to stand-out from other listings with aerial images and footage is undeniable, so it is understandable real estate agents and agencies want to incorporate this new tool into their sales and marketing offerings.

As discussed in the previous section, there are two ways agents and agencies can embrace this new aerial vison of properties. Contracting out the service to a Field Service Provider (FSP) or building out an sUAS program internally. The biggest deciding factor rests with the need to have a champion of this new technology within the business. This sUAS champion must be committed to researching, learning, implementing, and applying this new technology for the organization. As part of the decision process, consider some of the pros and cons to implementing an sUAS program.

PROs	CONs
• Full control of the use of sUAS as a tool ○ Quality control of images / video	• Investment in and management of: ○ UAV Equipment ○ UAS Software programs (i.e. fleet management)

○ Ability to react quickly for last minute projects

- Ability to grow and evolve the service offering unique services to shifting client needs
  ○ Ability to offer aerial services to generate new revenue streams
- Flexibility - ability to "move quickly" on last minute projects
- Assurance of consistency across projects
- Ensure safety expectations in the field are met
- Access & use of exciting new technology

- Upgrading or adding editing software programs
- Commitment to becoming or training someone within the business to become a certified remote pilot
- Commitment to staying up to date with FAA regulations, certification and airspace requirements
- Additional insurance (aviation specific) is required

To implement an sUAS program successfully, the real estate agency MUST have at least one person dedicated to researching, learning, implementing, and applying this new technology. A CHAMPION who will keep abreast of changes, including regulatory changes.

Adding an in-house sUAS program requires a commitment to this new sUAS technology and its safe application. Not only does it require an understanding of relevant regulations for the airspace being flown, it necessarily requires a familiarity and application of privacy, safety and risk management best-practices. With all the moving pieces, it's important to take it slow, fully define the implementation process, learn the technical skill of flying a UAV commercially, and ultimately offer the new sUAS service to end-clients.

So, it's been decided to standup an internal sUAS program within the real estate agency because there is a champion eager and willing to take on the challenge! GREAT! This section highlights particulars to set up an sUAS program.

Crawl: Understanding the World of UAV / sUAS a.k.a. Drones

Participating within the commercial sUAS (a.k.a. drones) industry means participating in a federally regulated industry; it's vital that key players within the organization implementing the sUAS program understand this. It is also the key to setting up a strong foundation to a sUAS program within the organization that is safe, efficient, and offers value.

First things first: What are all these names for drones?

- **RPAS** – Remotely Piloted Aerial System
- **UAV** – Unmanned Aerial Vehicle
- **UAS** – Unmanned Aircraft System
- **sUAS** – Small Unmanned Aircraft System
- **Hexacopter:** A multi-rotor aircraft having six rotors which adds redundancy in that it can lose any single engine and still maintain control to land. The Yuneec Typhoon H and H520 are an example of a hexacopter.
- **Multicopter:** A generic name for a drone with multiple propellers.
- **Quadcopter:** This is the most popular format for small UAVs, which four rotors positioned on a horizontal plane like a helicopter. Similar names include: *Quadricopter, Quadrocopter.* The most popular drone in this category is the DJI Phantom series or the Autel XStar.
- **Octocopters:** Are typically larger aircraft with eight rotors and are typically designed to carry a heavier payload. A good example of an Octocopter is the DJI S1000 or FREEFLY Alta 8 Drone

To further assist, there is a Glossary of Drone Terms at the back of this book.

Why is Commercial UAV (drone) use Federally regulated?

The long and short of it: **The FAA.** The FAA (Federal Aviation Administration) is responsible for the safety of civil aviation. As part of the Department of Transportation, their role is to ensure that anything in the air (ANYTHING above the ground) is safe. Per their website, their role is[1]:

- Regulating civil aviation to promote safety
- Encouraging and developing civil aeronautics, including new aviation technology
- Developing and operating a system of air traffic control and navigation for both civil and military aircraft
- Researching and developing the **National Airspace System** and civil aeronautics
- Developing and carrying out programs to control aircraft noise and other environmental effects of civil aviation
- Regulating U.S. commercial space transportation

The emphasis on **National Airspace System (NAS)** is the key. Commercial UAVs are flying within the NAS, sharing the air with helicopters, and airplanes (large & small). When flying a UAV in the United States, it is the pilot in command's (PIC) responsibility to understand and abide by the rules. (The same can be said about flying a UAV in most countries.)

For further details on understand-ing the regulations within the Com-mercial UAV industry, refer to the Chapter dedicated to this subject: "Understanding Regulation".

A quick overview follows.

---

[1] Federal Aviation Administration. 2016. "What we do." Retrieved Feb. 28, 2018 (https://www.faa.gov/about/mission/activities/).

Business / Commercial UAV Flight

The FAA definition of Commercial UAV Use includes

- Selling photos or videos taken from a UAS
- Using UAS to provide contract services, such as industrial equipment or factory inspection
- Using UAS to provide professional services, such as security or telecommunications
- Using UAS to monitor the progress of work the company is performing
- Professional real estate or wedding photography
- Professional cinema photography for a film or television production
- Providing contract services for mapping or land surveys

By definition, setting up an sUAS section within the real estate organization is commercial use of an sUAS.

Understanding Airspace Rules

Flying UAVs comes with the responsibility of understanding the rules of the sky. One of the most important aspects of this is understanding the airspace in which the UAV will fly. Following are a few key points to keep in mind before flying any project.

> ALWAYS CHECK YOUR AIRSPACE BEFORE FLYING YOUR sUAS!

Airports and Heliports

The general expectation is to avoid UAV flight within a five-mile radius around airports or heliports, however there are some exceptions and permission be granted from the FAA via a

process known as a waiver. The process of applying for a waiver with the FAA is well documented on their website, but it is not something that should be taken lightly. Understanding aviation law, risk mitigation, and having ample flight experience will support the waiver process.

Temporary Flight Restrictions/Wildfires

Temporary Flight Restrictions (TFRs) are put in place by the FAA to deal with special activities, (airshow, President visiting, sporting events, etc.) This classification also includes ongoing wildfires, sourced from the Department of Interior.

Prohibited or Restricted Airspace

These are highly sensitive areas where UAV flight are strictly prohibited. (i.e. White House or military installations). Steer clear of these areas.

Walk: Define sUAS Services Offered, Policy Procedure and Operations Manuals and getting 107 Certified

It's important to take it slow, define the implementation process, and finally, learn the new skill of flying a drone commercially. As this new tool becomes familiar, real agents will be ready to "walk".

Organizational processes become more complex when working with drones and this is why it is vital to take it slow and get it right the first time—before the organization and technical application grows.

This approach means starting small, proving the value drones can deliver to the company, and scaling operations after an initial proof of concept. This requires getting things right early on and building upon successes down the line.

> **Start slow; prove the ROI; then scale operations**

sUAS Services

First and foremost, the real estate business must determine what aerial services will be offered to clients. Gathering aerial images is not much different than taking ground photographs and video of real estate projects, the key to efficient imaging is in having a shot list or video script. Understanding and detailing what the finished product is (or service provided to the end-client) is key.

Check out the chapter focused on real estate shot lists for more ideas.

Updating the PPO

Similar to the remote pilot looking to add field services to their list of offerings (earlier in this chapter), a real estate organization must consider the importance of a business Policy, Procedure, and Operations manual (PPO). Ideally as a going concern business, the organization already has some documentation on expectations on how its day-to-day operations are managed, including safety and risk management, compliance to health and safety, legal liabilities, and management of issues that may have serious consequence.

Adding in a new, regulated technology into the organization's workflow requires that the policy, procedure and operational manual be updated accordingly. The sUAS program will require a playbook for the regulatory requirements, its equipment (hardware and software), pre-planning expectations, workflow for the job site, data

management, and aircraft and battery maintenance.

This new operations section becomes the foundation upon which the sUAS services provided can grow safely beyond a single pilot. Its purpose is to ensure consistency of sUAS flights, data capture for each project, expectations of staff (dress code, interactions, etc.), steps to incorporate safety in every flight/project, and risk management procedures when things go awry.

A reminder: The PPO is a *living document*. In other words, it is a document that necessarily needs to be reviewed and updated on a regular basis. It is recommended to have this living document review annually.

Earlier in this chapter, a high-level overview for a real estate structured PPO was shared. Here we zero in on a couple of key points to be added into an already existing document.

Policy, Procedure and Operation Manual for Real Estate Agencies

- Certification Cards of Pilots
  - Include all pilots flying for the organization
- sUAS Safety Policy
- Best Practices Compliance Statement
- List of relevant business documents
  - Real Estate Project Questionnaire
    - To create the statement of work and understand the scope of the project
  - Safety Checklists
    - Pre-planning
    - On-Site Planning
    - Post-Flight Data maintenance
  - Templates of Flight Announcements
    - Neighborhood announcements/flyers
    - HOA letters
    - Police letters
  - Waivers (if necessary)
  - Mutual NDA (if necessary)

- FAA Regulatory Guideline, Directions, Permissions and Approvals
  - Overview of FAA guidelines and expectations
  - Definitions NOTAMs/DROTAMs requirements
- Alcohol, Drug, Fatigue and Health Management
- Privacy
- Occupational Health & Safety
- Maintenance and Log Requirements
  - Pilot's Flight Logs
  - UAV Flight Logs & Maintenance
  - Battery Logs
- Operations Specific
  - Purpose
  - Persons Authorized
  - Area of Operations
  - Plan of Activities
    - Safety!
    - Preflight standards
    - Clearing the area
    - Announcements (Power, launch, land)
    - Weather maximums (aircraft-based)
    - Risk mitigation practices (powerlines, antenna lines, TV antenna, other obstacles)
  - Permission to Operate
    - Waiver requirements
    - Property owners
    - Law enforcement officials
    - Fire department officials

- ❏ Local, State and Federal government
- ○ Security
- ○ Briefing of Pilot/Production Personnel
- ○ Certification/Airworthiness
- ○ Pilot Personnel/Minimum Requirements
- ○ Communications
  - ❏ Interaction with home owners
    - ☆ Prepping the homeowner for the flight
      - ➡ Staging outside of home, yard, automobiles, windows/doors etc.
      - ➡ Time required for flight/ensure home owner does not enter nor leave home during flight
  - ❏ Interaction with neighbors
    - ☆ Forewarn with notices on doors
      - ➡ Notify them of flight areas
      - ➡ Ensure they understand what will be captured
      - ➡ Flight launch time/land time (duration)
- ○ Accident Notification
- ○ Recall/Stop Procedures
- ○ Aerobatic Competency
- ○ Duties and Responsibilities of Personnel
- ○ Specific UAS Flight Conduct
- ○ Importance of consistent flight & data capture

- ❏ Data Management & File Naming
- ❏ GPS Meta Data
- Document Revision Control Page

> **REMINDER: The Policy, Procedures, and Operations manual(s) are LIVING documents which need to be reviewed at least annually.**

Get 107 Certified

Before the organization can begin to offer aerial services captured with a sUAS, someone within the organization needs to assume responsibility to become the remote pilot in command. This manual goes into greater detail of what 107 certification means and the process to achieve the FAA certification for commercial UAV flight in the chapter focused on regulations.

Test and Train with Aircraft and Software Solutions that Fit the Real Estate Organization's Business Strategy

During the walking stage of building out the business, it's important that there is flexibility in trying a variety of equipment options and software solutions. This step is all about research, testing, and researching some more. Research the equipment options, what are the pros/cons of each small unmanned aerial system (sUAS); what's their ease of use? Limitations? Expansion ability?

> **Research, test. Repeat. Find the right equipment (and software) solution to meet the business strategy.**

This manual goes into greater detail on the questions to be answered when looking to make the final equipment investment in a sUAS. See the chapter on equipment selection for more specifics.

While "walking", take the time to fly a variety of UAVs in the market. Join a Meetup group, connect with a local retailer and have them demonstrate the options available. Test a variety of software solutions that meet the business needs; many solutions offer a free 30-day trial before a commitment is required. Take advantage of the free trial periods and put it to work. Once the kinks have been worked out, it's time to finalize the business' PPO.

Run: Equipment Selection, Practice, and Flight Training

The new real estate service has researched, tested, and defined; the agency's PPO has been updated. It's time to RUN and begin offering the new aerial services, which means it's time to commit to an aircraft to fly, software programs for aircraft maintenance and management, data collection, and video/photo editing.

As the sUAS Services are being sold, it is important to keep "the bottom line" in mind when offering the service. As a new offering (and new pilot), it does make sense to offer the

services at an affordable rate to generate revenue, even taking losses from time to time on key projects that will increase the value of the agency's portfolio and the remote pilot's experience. That said, it is easy to be swept into the excitement of flying a "cool gig" only later to find out how much time was invested on getting the job done was a negative cashflow to the company. The process of offering sUAS as a service is a learning process and it's vital that profitability is scrutinized. As projects are completed and the portfolio built, a better understanding of the local area's requirements will be revealed. Keep focused on the hours spent on pre-planning a flight, flying (how efficient are you in the field?), and post-production management of images and footage collected. Like all new skills, as experience is built up, so too will the efficiency of each of the project steps.

One way to develop skills quickly is to take a training course with professionals (you don't know what you don't know) and of course, practice!

> Keep track of the hours spent pre-planning, planning, and processing each project to get a better sense of ROI.

One final note: be sure to update the business' PPO with changes to the sUAS process, pricing, and expectations for each sUAS project.

Aviation Insurance

As with any business venture, insurance is not legally required, yet no prudent business person would consider operating without insurance.

Offering sUAS as a service means also ensuring that the agency is covered with aviation insurance for the remote pilot and aircraft of choice. It is extremely rare that the business insurance will cover aviation activity of any kind but take the time to call the insurance carrier and ask questions. It is possible they may have a rider to add to the current insurance being provided.

Additional details can be found later in this manual on the two primary forms of aviation insurance available; Liability and Hull. Please be sure to read the section on insurance for additional details for more details. Suffice it to say, while it is not (currently) a requirement, it is good business practice to have aviation insurance for all commercial UAS activities.

Scope of sUAS Projects – New Service for Real Estate Agents & Agencies

Following are a list of ways the agency can quote for sUAS as a service. The complexity of a project will be dependent upon the sUAS champion within the organization and what support team is available to him/her. (i.e. Is the remote pilot of the agency expected to process the images/footage, or is there someone in the office will be responsible for that step?). It is also important to clearly define what the final product will be for the client to avoid any conflicting expectations. To do so, it is suggested that a Scope of Work (SOW) is shared with the client.

- Define the entire Scope of Work (SOW) with the client
  - Expected/Suggested Shot list
    - Aerial
    - Interiors integrated into the final product
  - Discuss a plan of action (prepping the home for aerial and interior shots)

- Waiver Requirements – Are the required waivers complete/available? Can one be rented from a pilot owning the required waiver? Alternatively, is there time to time to wait for a waiver application to be filed and approved?
  - ○ Filing for local airspace waivers is a good pro-active idea to do

As an agency adding sUAS as a service, determining the right price point for each project is similar to an FSP offering the service. Be sure to check out the earlier chapter detailing how to bid on a project for a variety of ways to offer aerial services to clients. Keep in mind that how the service is priced out is likely to shift as the pilot gains experience.

Below is the suggested best practice for offering the aerial service as a real estate agent/agency.

Method of Pricing	Pro	Con
Content Produced: **Photos**	• Pricing focuses on specific output needs to the client • (Image Size, Resolution, Editing / Retouching needs and quantity of Images) • Ability to offer a variety of price-point packages to the client	• Remote pilot must become a confident photo editor and understand the time required for managing images • Additional training may be required

Content Produced: Videos	• Pricing focuses on specific output needs to the client (Video length, music/graphic overlay, etc.) • Ability to offer a variety of price-point packages to the client	• Remote pilot must become a confident video editor and understand the time invested for cutting video together • Additional training may be required

But most importantly, do not undersell the value of the service provided. The business can only thrive once it goes beyond breaking even.

DO NOT UNDERSELL THE SERVICES PROVIDED!

FLY: Going Beyond sUAS Implementation

Now that the sUAS equipment and software workflow is implemented into the real estate sUAS business strategy, the next step is to keep focused on how this new tool can continue to add to the business' differentiation and ultimately the bottom line. The key is going beyond the basics, honing both flight skills and staying informed with changes within the sUAS industry and the technology.

Ultimately the key to success is two-fold: continue to do research and continue to learn.

Continue to Add to the UAS Catalogue of Skills – Develop Pilot Skills

As a new remote pilot, it can be challenging to capture "the easy shots" off the shot list. The more flight time a pilot has, managing a variety of situations and environments, skills and confidence advance. Keep with it. Push the comfort zone (safely!). Try new angles, new pans, new flythrough shots. Don't be afraid of trying new things. Some of the new footage/images will be further developed, practiced, and incorporated into the shot list. Others will quickly be discarded. This is a trial and error learning process which, as a remote pilot helps hone flight techniques and confidence.

Alternatively, taking a class with a recognized pilot-instructor can help speed up the learning process. It is highly recommended to take at least one practical flight course to learn specific flight techniques (many of which are noted later in this manual). Reading about them vs. *flying* the noted techniques are very different; having experience pilot explain the moves physically promotes a speedier learning process.

Continue to Add to the UAS Catalogue of Skills – Continue to Develop Content Produced

Real estate is about marketing a property – to sell it, or rather, make it look enticing enough to buy. In other words, the aerial content being created is used to *market* the property in question. Earlier it was suggested to work with a shot list (or template) to streamline each project's time in the field, which may mean there is little creativity built into the process. Now that we're "flying" with the sUAS implementation within the agency, it's time to add back the spice of creativity.

The best way to ensure aerial images captured remain "fresh" is to continue to add new perspectives into the end-product being produced. That means trying new flight techniques, but it also means incorporating the aerial images/footage into ground-based images/footage. The challenging part of placing multiple media captures together is ensuring that the video pacing aligns. This manual goes into further detail pacing real estate videos in a later chapter.

Here are some additional suggestions to keep adding unique perspectives into the service provided, as a remote pilot and as a content producer.

1. Continue to try (and master) new flight techniques (See the advanced flight section for ideas)
   - ○ Experience pilots should build upon their flight techniques; more complicated flight patterns and combinations can create more exciting content such as:
     - i. *Precision Flying* – get closer to a key subject area
     - ii. *Pass Thru Flying* – fly through two buildings before revealing the aerial view
2. When creating videos and images for clients, continue to add new editing stylings with gained experience and confidence (See editing chapter for examples)
   - ○ There is a myriad of tutorials online to learn how to edit images and cut video together, including some on fun and interesting techniques.

- ○ Consider taking in-class workshops or attend a tradeshow offering a variety of educational sessions dedicated to increasing skills and efficiency with photo and video editing.
    - i. NAB, Adobe Video World, SXSW, InFocus are all great conferences to attend to learn about creativity, video editing techniques, and real-world experience by working in groups.
    - ii. Online courses will also walk through editing video: Lynda.com; udemy.com are paid courses, but browse through Youtube for insights too (PremiereGal on Youtube is one of many examples)

3. Going beyond the aerial content
    - ○ Integrate the end-product with ground footage and images

    - ○ Include access to virtual tours, etc.
    - ○ Add a music bed to the produced content

The importance of keeping the sUAS service offerings current and unique is key to the real estate agency's differentiation in the market. Keeping ahead of competition will offer success within a quickly advancing sUAS service provider industry.

Continue to Research and Update PPO

It's important to be a part of the UAS community, be it local, state or federal. Be a part of the conversation to grow and adapt efficiently as the industry grows.

— Jennifer Pidgen

As mentioned earlier, sUAS as a tool is changing quickly. Manufacturers (hardware and software), resellers (third party accessories), service providers (insurance, FSPs, fleet management), and national regulations (FAA) are a shifting environment. Once the sUAS program is off the ground, it is very important for the company's sUAS champion to keep informed on new offerings, shifts in technology, and most importantly, current regulation requirements as a commercial remote pilot. The key, as mentioned before is research. Join a Facebook or LinkedIn group online which speaks to commercial remote pilots (there are many to choose from, some local, some national, some international); join a group on Facebook/LinkedIn focused on legal issues within the UAS industry (fewer available, but those available are quite active in discussions on that is happening in the legal/regulatory landscape. Get involved with local Meetup groups. Be a part of the commercial UAS conversation.

Finally, as changes are made to the sUAS service workflow, it's important to revisit the organization's PPO. (i.e. changes, or additions to the business workflow, or additions to the equipment). This document is a *living document*, meaning that it needs to be updated as changes are made within the organization. Realistically this doesn't happen in real time, which is why it is recommended to schedule an annual review the business' PPO. If time and resources allow, PPOs should (ideally) be reviewed bi-annually, especially in such a fast-moving industry as UAS.

> **REMINDER: A PPO is a living document; it needs to be updated when changes within the organization occur.**

Hidden side of Planning

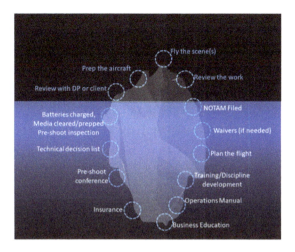

There is so much more to crafting the final product then simply showing up to fly the project! Be prepared. Pre-plan, site plan, and manage each project carefully.

Choosing an sUAS

When making decisions about which aircraft to use for real estate work, there are a few points that should be considered. sUAS are tools, and like anything else, choosing the right tool for the job can make a significant impact on hard vs moderate work or frustration vs. feeling content with the workflow. Asking a few questions will help determine which tool is best for a specific workflow, area, or goal.

> **sUAS are tools. To choose the correct tool, it's necessary to define what its purpose will be.**

Budget is typically a first consideration. Determine the budget range and add 20% to the overall expectation. Accessories, training, and parts will quickly expend additional dollars. Remember, a new business is being started, and unanticipated expenses are common. Plan, but do not be surprised when expenses go a bit beyond the planned cost. Plan on spending a minimum of $4000 for the most basic sUAS for Business package.

Ask questions regarding the operations. Answers to these questions will help determine the best model(s) for specific environments and workflows. For example:

Is the region a high-wind region? If so, a hexacopter is something to consider. Hexacopter (six motors) in virtually every situation, will fly with greater stability than a quadcopter (four motors). hexacopter also offer the value of a redundant motor in the event a prop is damaged in flight or a motor fails for any reason. Most hexacopter can fly with reasonable  stability with only five operational motors.

Is the region a wet/damp area? If so, a UAS that offers water resistance should be very high on the consideration list. There are many third-party companies across the industry that have the ability to water-treat most aircraft systems. Is the region high-altitude? Cold or hot to the extreme? If so, special props, heat packs, cooling system, or other special accessories may be required.

Consider portability in the product selection process. If the company vehicle is a compact car, then a large aircraft in a hard case is likely not the best solution. Hard cases are essential to the professional pilot who is traveling from house to business to commercial site capturing photos or video. The hard case takes the bangs and bumps of the road, so the aircraft does not have to. A hard case goes a long way to ensuring the airworthiness of the aircraft pursuant to AC107-2. Cases also help prevent damage to propellers, protect cameras and other related gear.

> There is no "one-size-fits-all" aircraft. Finding the right tool will take some research and testing against required outputs.

In short, there is no "one-size-fits-all" aircraft. Certainly, there are systems that are more versatile than others, while there are some aircraft that for most workflows may fall into the "too small" vs "too large" categories. For example, pilots working predominantly with commercial properties may find a larger aircraft is required for carrying heavier DSLR cameras to better match imagery from inside the property, while residential real estate content creators will find that smaller aircraft are ideally suited for capture of the areas surrounding the home. Residential pilots may find that a larger aircraft is more difficult to store, set up and slower to deploy, making them less nimble. This may be an important consideration for example, when working in a closed community or HOA and a narrow window of permission has been granted for flight within the HOA.

NOISE

sUAS prop volumes may significantly vary in loudness from one to another. When working in residential areas, this can be a valuable consideration. A hexacopter is virtually always less noisy than a quad, while a dual axis octacopter is simply very, very loud. In the current political and social climate, reducing the footprint of the sUAS as much as possible is of great benefit to most pilots. A quiet sUAS generally draws less attention, resulting in fewer persons being aware of the aircraft. In a quiet neighborhood, a quiets UAS may provide fewer interruptions.

Again, consider the environment where one will be working when choosing the aircraft.

PAYLOADS/SENSORS

"Payload" is a descriptive name for whatever the aircraft might carry. "Sensor" is a form of payload as well. "Sensor" generally refers to a camera system of some sort. Sensors may be standard cameras, Light Detection and Ranging (LiDAR), Normalized Difference Vegetation Index (NDVI), thermal/infrared, sonar, and other systems. For real estate use, sensors generally include a wide angle RGB camera in the 16mm to 50mm focal length (35mm equivalent), and some pilots may opt for a thermal sensor for roof/building efficiency inspections. LiDAR is primarily used for large scale construction, forestry, or other areas that benefit from laser-measuring. NDVI is a sensor designed for measuring state of vegetation, for example, a farmer might use NDVI to measure and monitor crop health.

Ensure the payload/camera has the ability to accept filters. Although the "why" is discussed in another portion of this book, do not purchase any aircraft that does not have the ability to attach a filter to the camera lens. There simply is no way to effectively capture images without using filters, particularly when shooting at hours outside of shortly after sunrise and shortly before sunset. Most sUAS cameras can accept filters somehow or another, yet there are some that cannot. **Be absolutely certain of filter ability prior to purchasing an aircraft or camera system.**

> **Be sure that your chosen aircraft will accept filters to ensure effective capture of images.**

GIMBAL

Does the system have a detachable gimbal/camera operation device? In real estate, this is a valuable tool for allowing the UAS to "fly" through the residence or business. Transiting/editing video that has smooth flight, shifting to jerky, hand-held movement inside a building will be jarring to viewers. Some systems, such as the GoPro Karma and the DJI Inspire offer included or optional hand-held gimbal accessories, enabling the pilot or producer to maintain an identical 'feel' or flow to video captured inside the building to that of footage captured outdoors.

The GoPro Karma-Grip is a low-cost hand-held solution that functions only with the GoPro camera products.

The DJI Osmo is made for either their proprietary cameras that fly on the Inspire 1/2/3 aircraft, or for mobile phone use.

Yuneec offers a handheld system for their older cameras that uses a mobile phone for previewing what is being recorded at the camera.

Landing Gear

Most sUAS, particularly consumer products, have a fixed camera system that cannot be changed out for a different camera. Essentially, one learns to fly the aircraft to the best abilities of the camera system. Yet other systems may offer the ability to change payloads, allowing the aircraft to be versatile in both use and efficiency on-site. Large format aircraft with adjustable large gimbals may also be capable of switching out lenses, carrying multiple cameras at once, etc. Commercial real estate may require some of these light-medium lifter aircraft that might carry a large DSLR with large lens for photos with a smaller camera for video use, and yet perhaps a third, smaller camera for pilot POV.

Aircraft that have fixed payloads (cameras that cannot be removed) generally have fixed landing gear as well. This may work well for some, yet there is a significant value found in articulated landing gear, or landing gear that fold out of the camera's view during flight. Some sUAS offer a constant rotation of 360 degrees, while others are locked into a 355-degree rotation that cannot quite go all the way around. Retractable or articulated legs allow these sorts of cameras to look around while the aircraft is stable in one area, providing for a smoother rotation during hovers, or extremely creative moves while the aircraft arcs in the opposite direction of a rotating (yawing) camera. Essentially, retractable legs allow the pilot to rotate the camera from the forward view to a rearward view without the legs/landing gear of the aircraft getting into the shot.

> Fixed payloads offer less flexibility. Articulating landing gear can offer full 360 degree views.

When landing gear are seen in the image like this, it's very difficult to crop/correct in post. Shooting 4K will help (when delivering in HD); the correct remedy is to ensure legs are never in the frame.

Without the ability to retract the landing gear/legs, the camera on the sUAS must face forward and turning camera angles must be managed by the yaw of the aircraft.

Automation

Automation (think "AutoPilot") can play a large role in achieving successful content, be it video or still photographs. Automation is a means of controlling the aircraft hands-free, and allows the pilot to plan the exact altitude, angle, speed, and motion of the aircraft prior to arriving on-site. A pilot might sit down at a computer screen with the home owner or realtor to preplan, and pre-visualize the flight using desktop planning software, so that all parties are informed as to exactly where the aircraft will fly, where the camera is pointing, angle of flight to/from any specific points of interest, etc. Additionally, automated flight makes it possible to easily ensure perfect circles around points of interest such as interesting features of the home or property, capturing 3D scan information, or smooth orbits of items of regional interest.

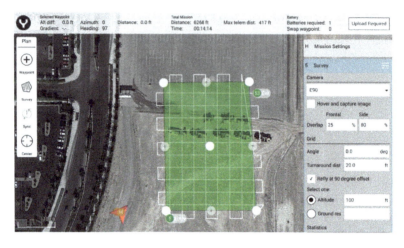

Litchi, a mission planning software compatible with DJI drones, is a great add-on. Yuneec DataPilot is a very efficient mission planning tool that functions on Mac, Windows, or Android systems. DJI GSC is DJI's Ground Control Station software for iOS devices. All three applications are relatively quick to learn and implement.

Automation for orthomosaic mapping allows content creators to capture hundreds (or thousands) of images of a specific area, at equal points in distance or time, that are then stitched into one large image/map. This is a valuable means of showing the home with deep detail, particularly on roofs or yards that contain great detail.

Automation also allows flight in exceptionally tight areas where less experienced pilots may be nervous about flying at slow speeds, or in areas where wind funnels or turbulence may be better managed through automation than manual flight.

Another benefit of automated flight is one of repetition. Automated flight plans may be stored/archived for later retrieval, loaded to the aircraft, and precision-point re-fly the same area. Moreover, flights during a construction phase of property may be repetitively flown at specific intervals, allowing for the creation of time-lapse construction video or still images with motion.

Applications such as DroneDeploy ™, Pix4D ™, and some of the other mapping/rendering tools also include mission planning software.

Pix4D's mission planning application supports Yuneec, DJI, and Parrot UAS.

DroneDeploy's mission planning application supports DJI products.

TABLET VS PHONE

Most sUAS utilize either a built-in tablet or a cradle for a user-choice tablet, used for not only preview of what the airborne camera is viewing/recording, but also an interface for controlling portions of the sUAS. Essentially, the tablet or phone interface is the dashboard of the aircraft. Systems that allow user to choose an external tablet are variable in what size tablet or phone may be used for system operation. Although it is tempting to use a mobile phone for sUAS operations, it is not advisable. The video display is the "window" out of the aircraft. Any Part 61 pilot (manned aircraft) will express the preference for a large windshield, no different than many drivers prefer large windshields on their automobile. A larger tablet/interface allows the user to see detail more clearly, relieves eye strain, reduces the length of screen-scan while piloting, and allows a more efficient cadence when viewing "screen, sky, scan".

"Screen, sky, scan" refers to the rhythm of looking at the interface/video preview screen (tablet), looking at the UAS in the sky, and scanning for obstacles or threats in the sky surrounding the aircraft.

A typical cadence might be like a waltz; Screen 2-3, Sky 2-3, Scan 2-3 1, 2, 3, Screen 2-3, Sky 2-3 Scan 2-3, 1, 2, 3, Screen...and so forth. All experienced pilots have a cadence of some sort. Find a cadence/tempo that works best in your conditions and stick with it with rare exception.

The Yuneec ST16S provides a built-in 7" Android™ tablet, saving battery charging time and eliminating the need for an additional device.

A larger screen (we recommend a minimum of 7") also allows for greater view of flight control feedback such as altitude, speed, distance from pilot/operator, compass heading. Small screens make these console displays much more difficult to read and staring or squinting at the screen in bright sunlight while the UAS is flying is never a good idea. This is why cadences are used, to help remind pilots to constantly be rotating eyes between the aircraft and the screen, while searching the sky for obstacles or threats.

A larger screen also reduces the necessity of a Visual Observer.

> **Consider a field monitor for detailed viewing of image capture in the field.**

An alternative to a larger screen mounted on the remote-control system, would be a larger monitor connected either via WiFi or HDMI, on a table or stand that might be viewed by a visual observer, pilot, or homeowner, or real estate agent on-scene, so that everyone is aware of what the source footage looks like.

DJI's Crystal Sky technology is very bright and can be readily seen in sunlight without using a hood or sunshade.

Some sUAS allow for a pilot and separate camera operator controlling only the camera. In these instances, a pilot might use a 7" tablet while the camera operator uses a 10" monitor for control of the camera, and to better visualize camera movement. When it comes to visualizing surroundings, the larger the window, the easier it is to see what the aircraft sees.

Regardless of what sort of tablet is used for operations, it is no replacement for eyes on the aircraft. FAA requirements for commercial operations without a waiver are Visual Line of Sight/VLOS. This means that the unaided human eye must be capable of seeing the aircraft in the sky at all times by the pilot and/or designated Visual Observer.

> Monitors and screens do NOT replace the need for EYES on the aircraft. The sUAS must always be visual line of sight. (VLOS)

Battery Life

Battery life on the tablet is another concern. Some tablets have poor battery life while others have long-life batteries. DJI also offers their own tablet that allows for interchangeable batteries.

A common way of supplying additional power to the tablets / phones is using a battery bank to help recharge the tablet or phone.

Heat

Heat is another consideration. On more than one occasion, pilots have found themselves "burned out" of a job because their tabled is incapable of managing ambient heat. Our team predominantly works in the Southwest where summer temperatures climb well above 100°F, well beyond the operational limitations of many tablets. Yuneec has an air-cooled Ground Station Controller that offers a fan-cooled, ventilated control that works well in extreme heat. Alternatively, Hoodman produces a cooling pad for most tablets that has replaceable cooling inserts.

The Yuneec ST16S has an inducted-air cooling system, allowing the Ground Station Controller to operate in very hot areas.

Pilot/Camera Operator Systems

"Commercial" or Enterprise sUAS often offer the ability to operate the aircraft and camera separately, requiring two operators/pilots (the person controlling the aircraft must hold an FAA certification). Having this ability provides the pilot freedom to focus solely on the aircraft and its surroundings while the camera operator is solely focused on well, focus, direction, and angle of the camera. In most instances, the camera operator and pilot are situated near each other so that they may communicate. Some operations use "closed-loop" communication systems where the two operators wear headsets with boom microphones, shutting out communications from other persons. Frequently, the pilot will also have a feed from the local Air Traffic Control (ATC) in one ear while listening to the camera operator in the other ear.

While it certainly is not necessary to listen ATC during operations in Class G airspace, it is a good habit to get into during even normal residential operations; be aware of aviation activity in the area of operation. In controlled airspace, listening to ATC *may* serve as the FAA requirement of "being in contact with ATC," depending on the airspace and area requirements. Our team has found it extremely beneficial to use a Bluetooth earwig while monitoring local flights over ATC app.

COMPATIBILITY

When choosing a sUAS, compatibility with other systems or software is an important consideration. Choosing an aircraft designed for one sort of work may not offer output formats compatible with some types of software. The overall goal is to identify and select and aircraft that is not only sized correctly and provides a comfortable control surface in specific circumstances, that might deploy quickly and is easily transportable, that is also compatible with real estate-related software.

> Consider the full workflow before choosing the aircraft. Ensure that all the pieces of the toolset work together.

Some questions to consider;

- Does the camera output RAW or DNG file formats? Which does my software prefer?
- Does the camera output HEVC or .mp4 file formats? Which does my software prefer?

Speed from post-flight to final product output whether a report, map, model, sales-focused video, elevation inspection, etc. is a very important consideration. Time is money and the more time spent on post-production/post-flight, the less opportunity there is to be flying. The money is in the quality of flight and quality of output; these are the two areas on which prospective pilots should focus if generating revenue is the goal.

CAMERA SETUP

There are different setups for photo and video uses; in this section we'll look at them as separate components.

Video Resolution

Most of the cameras found on sUAS systems today are very capable of capturing great footage/content and the majority of systems manufactured in 2017 or later are capable of shooting 4K footage.

> **4K is four times the number of pixels of High Definition, a format slowly falling by the wayside.**

4K carries some significant benefits over shooting in HD, yet not all pilots/producers are going to have a computer that can manage 4K video files. It's easy to put the cart before the horse when it comes to 4K. Shooting in 4K without a computer/

software capable of handling 4K files will result in slow, frustrating editing experiences, and the length of time to process, edit, and output files from a 4K source may potentially offset the value of the greater resolution. Later in this book, we'll dive into video editing applications; they are not all created equal. There are software tools that will allow even a slower, older computer to properly manage 4K files. And there are software tools that will struggle with 4K files on even the fastest/latest/greatest computer system not configured for video editing.

In different terms, consider a semi-trailer in the desert filled with gold bricks, but no tractor with which to pull them out of the desert so the bricks can be put into a bank or spent. The trailer is the 4K file, but without a computer that might best harness and move the files around...the value of the 4K file is lost.

If the computer can process HD yet struggles with 4K, many cameras are capable of resolutions of 2.7K. This is a "middle" resolution that allows post-production options (assuming delivery in HD) while not being nearly as "heavy" as 4K.

In most situations, output will be 1920x1080 or some derivative of HD standards. Capturing at higher resolutions does offer flexibility in post-production, and both 4K and 2.7k video are viable options for capture.

Choose wisely. Download 4K HEVC or 4K .mp4 files and try them on the computer that will be used for editing purposes to better understand the formats. This will be discussed in greater depth in the "Editing" section of this book. There are downloadable samples of all video formats in many locations on the internet. Download and experiment to determine the best resolutions and framerates for available computer systems and software. Not all software manages the footage the same; experiment with various software if no in-house format exists.

> **Not all software manages the footage the same; experiment with various software programs.**

With all this having been said, shoot in 4K if there is a computer available that can manage the files. Doing so allows so many more options in post-production, it is well worth the additional effort it takes to capture these large format files.

Original 4K image, uncropped and uncorrected

Cropped/Corrected 4K image, in HD. Note the image is 1920 x 900, a very common wide-screen delivery aspect ratio.

Video Framerate

Virtually all the 4K and HD camera systems are able to capture video at multiple framerates. Which is the best for individual operations? Like most other aspects of sUAS, "it depends."

Available framerates (expressed in frames per second, or "fps) are typically 24p, 25p, 30p, 48p, 50p, 60p, and 120p. Some systems are capable of shooting as many as 240 frames per second.

Here's a breakdown of framerates and common uses.

24 fps /24p	This framerate is used predominantly by film-makers that have experience moving cameras slowly and with proper stability so as to not cause eye jitter in viewers. This is not a useful format for most real estate uses, inspections, etc. 24p also reduces light capture, and should never be used in low light settings without advance screen tests for noise and motion issues. There is one major benefit to 24p; it is 25% smaller in file size, and ideal for video delivery in large format, to reduce streaming file size.
25p	25p is an EU standard that is rarely seen in North America. Similar to 24P, video experience on the ground is highly recommended before using this format for aerial operations. Using this format in the Americas will result in light strobing due to lighting and frames being out of sync. Fly slowly for best results. In earlier years, this framerate was referred to as "PAL." The "PAL" format died with the advent of HD.

30p	As the most common, basic framerate in North America, this is a good go-to frame rate for general purpose video capture. This framerate is in sync with 60Hz electrical lighting found both indoors and outdoors, preventing light-stutter generated from frames and electrical cycles being out of sync.
	In earlier years, this framerate was referred to as "NTSC." The "NTSC" format died with the advent of HD.
48p	48p is a relative newcomer to filmmaking. Only highly experienced operators will want to work with this framerate, as it can create "flutter" that appears to be surreal, and not necessarily in a good way, when not properly managed.
50p	50p is double the framerate of 25p. It provides for very smooth motion, much better transition to half-speed motion, and will become the EU standard in a reasonably short period of time. It is the prevalent capture rate for EU sports in HD. The EU has been very slow to adopt 4K for broadcast.
60p	60p is double the framerate of 30p. It provides for very smooth motion, much cleaner transfer to half-speed motion, and will become the EU standard in a reasonably short period of time. It is the prevalent capture rate for North American sports in HD and 4K.

120p	120p is a common framerate when extreme slow motion is desired. This is a common framerate for new pilots who have not yet learned to smoothly fly. Most small format UAS cameras reduce the overall image resolution to achieve this much higher framerate.

> **Pilots new to video shoot at a resolution of either 2.7K and framerate of 30fps OR if slow motion is required, 60fps.**

It is recommended that pilots new to video, or not matching external cameras, shoot at a resolution of either 2.7K and a framerate of 30fps (25fps in EU). If slow motion is to be created in post-production, capture at a frame rate of 60fps (50fps in EU). File sizes will be large. Use U3 cards.

SETTING UP THE GROUND STATION CONTROL (GSC)

The GSC is the heart of every UAS system and taking the time to become familiar with the GSC is time well-spent. Going beyond the basics of setting up metric vs Imperial and acres vs rods, dive into the way the joysticks feel, the travel of the various knobs and dials, and become deeply familiar with the controls to the point that they can be operated without looking at the GSC. There will be times in high-stress, where there will not be opportunity to glance at the controls. Having solid muscle memory may make the difference between operational success and failure when an emergency arises.

> Go beyond familiar with your GSC; know its abilities inside and out. Muscle memory will serve well in an emergency.

Many GSC have menus that allow for custom operations and custom "feel" to each control. Changing these menu settings and parameters allow users to be more efficient and typically safer in operational control due to the personal touch. When these parameters are changed, spend time re-learning the touch of the controls. Anytime any component of the system changes, whether it's the tablet, menu settings, shoulder harness, or other shift in the norm of the control system, spend time re-familiarizing and re-learning the controls.

Setting up the GSC For Two Operators

Dual operator systems can be very useful. Previously discussed, one pilot controls flight-only while the other pilot (or camera operator) manages only the camera.

A camera operator controlling a second GSC that is controlling only the camera does not require an FAA Remote Pilot Certification (RPC). The individual piloting the flight of the aircraft is required to hold an FAA RPC. However, it is common sense that the camera operator be able to take over control of the aircraft in case of any sort of emergency.

> The individual piloting the flight of the aircraft is required to hold a current 107 remote pilot certification or be directly observed by a holder of a 107 certificate.

As mentioned previously, set up the pilot remote to pilot specification. In a dual remote scenario, the pilot remote should be clearly marked as the Pilot Remote. The secondary remote should be marked as Camera Remote.

While it is very easy to swap one remote system for another in most systems, set up time in the field goes much more rapidly when each remote is task-specific. For example, the camera remote may be set up with slower dials or rotation for smoother movement, or joysticks programmed for intuitive camera movement. Perhaps the camera controller will hold a very large tablet or be connected directly to a freestanding monitor. In some instances, the camera operator may be operating from inside a van or control truck while the pilot is outside the control area with eyes on the aircraft. These setups are always best done in advance not only to save time, but also to identify any technical issues with equipment.

Practice flight with a dual operator system in a variety of environments ranging from multi-story buildings to high winds with obstacles. Aligning two operators is much more difficult than it may seem, as each individual may have different ideas of capturing the shot. Planning the shot well in advance goes without saying, and a strong team will develop terms and operational nomenclature to aid in the planning and execution of multi-operator missions. Again, muscle memory will play a significant role in successful flight operations and mission execution.

Muscle memory has been used synonymously with motor learning, which is a form of procedural memory (unconscious memory) that involves consolidating a specific motor task into memory through repetition. When a movement is repeated over time, a long-term muscle memory is created for that task, eventually allowing it to be performed without conscious effort. This process decreases the need for attention and creates maximum efficiency within the motor and memory systems.

Batteries, Props, And Other Necessary Accessories

An sUAS is more than just the aircraft and GSC. Having spare parts will go a long way to building out the confidence required to fly in challenging areas. Like the Boy Scout motto says, "Be Prepared."

> **Be prepared.** Consider the environment (hot/cold); Have extra props; ensure the safety of the sUAS crew.

Batteries

Batteries are the fuel that keep the sUAS flying. A professional operator will carry at minimum, five batteries, while most will carry at least 10. In any event, multiple batteries are always required with the average sUAS battery providing approximately 20 minutes of flight, conditions dependent. If using batteries outside manufacturer brands, be certain that any batteries used are authorized by the manufacturer. Otherwise, batteries may fall into a violation of AC 107-2. Calculate flight times per battery at 75% of the total battery life. Never fly beyond equipment warning points. Most systems and batteries are designed to warn at approximately 30% and return to home/RTH at approximately 20%, leaving time for a safe descent and landing.

> Third party batteries may be more affordable, but ensure their use is authorized by the manufacturer!

Heat & Cold

The quoted battery flight time from manufacturers is based on an ideal environment. When in the field working on a project, heat is an environmental factor that will affect the flight time on a battery. In higher temperatures (and check your aircrafts manual for specifics on ideal temperatures), batteries will have a lower than expected flight times. One way of keeping batteries cooler, is using a cooler bag with freezer inserts/ice packs. One word of warning: be sure to use ice packs that are non-condensating, or have the ice packs wrapped in towels, in a zip lock bag. This will keep any moisture from the melting ice packs away from the batteries.

On the other hand, cold is also an environmental consideration when operating aircraft. Like higher than ideal temperatures, cold temperatures will also affect the decrease the output of batteries. One way to generate the manufacturer's quoted flight times is to ensure that batteries are kept at the manufacturer's recommended temperatures (typically room temperature). One way to do this, in extreme cold, is to have an insulated box (a cooler would work) with a warming device within it. (Hot pockets, heated bean-bag, or even a USB-heated article of clothing would work.)

Wind and Accessories

Flying in windier conditions will also decrease the performance of batteries. The more wind, the harder motors are working to keep the aircraft steady. Outside of being aware of battery consumption being quicker, there really isn't much that can be done to prevent the decrease in performance.

Adding accessories to any aircraft (additional lighting as an example) will also affect the performance of batteries. It is recommended to check the aircraft's manual before installing third party accessories. Once installed, be note of changes in battery consumption for awareness when using the modified aircraft on a project.

Multi-charger

Large projects are far more efficient with multi battery, high-speed chargers. Pictured above is not an optimal charging solution. Cube-type chargers may actually damage batteries; be sure to test cells and charge level before flying. For Yuneec batteries, it is recommended to purchase a third-party voltage meter to test batteries before flight.

Multi-bay chargers such as those available from manufacturers like Venom Power, EVPeak, and other quality chargers should be a serious consideration. Battery management is critical in UAS operations. Typically, manufacturer's single/

cube chargers are not fast enough, and cannot charge multiple batteries at once.

This charger will rapidly charge or discharge up to four batteries at once, while also conditioning batteries.

Multichargers generally include the ability to discharge batteries for long-term storage. Batteries are best stored between 35-50% of capacity (consult UAS manual for manufacturer recommendation). Multichargers make this tedious task more efficient and hassle-free, leaving the pilot free to accomplish other tasks without needing to babysit discharging batteries. The same can be said for charging; batteries should not be placed on low-grade chargers and allowed to sit once fully charged. A high-grade charger will shut down the charging bay once the inserted battery reaches full charge.

> **Batteries are best stored between 35-50% of capacity**

Other Battery Considerations

• Never leave batteries charging while unattended. Once batteries are charged, remove them from the charger

- Identify a method of indicating which batteries are charged and which aren't. Smart batteries are great, yet from 15 feet away from the battery, it's impossible to know whether the battery is charged or not.
  - A popular method of working with batteries is to:
    - Place discharged batteries upside down on the battery pad
    - Batteries that are upside right are charged and ready to fly

There are also termi-nal caps for various sorts of batteries. Green caps identify charged batteries, while red caps indi-cate discharged batteries.

When travelling via commercial airline, these battery terminal covers are handy as terminals are required to be covered.

> **Batteries need to be replaced every 250-350 charging cycles.**

- Be certain that all batteries are *numbered*, and each *charge cycle is logged* (this is a FAR).
- Batteries need to be replaced every 250-350 cycles (Manufacturers have recommendations, so knowing how many charges have been placed on each battery is valuable information and may be needed in the event of an FAA ramp check.
  - Again, the type of charger used may impact the lifecycle of batteries.

PROPELLERS

This should be self-evident, yet it seems that many pilots don't consider the many reasons for carrying at least a full set of propellers plus two.

This propeller is not suited for flight, and could cause an incident

Consider this:

A pilot who has only enough props for flight may fly differently than a pilot who knows they have additional props in the box. Being afraid of ruining a flight due to a damaged prop may affect confidence, and overall affect the quality of the operation or mission execution.

Props are easily chipped/damaged during landings when small rocks may be flipped due to propwash, dirt or foreign objects on window ledges, trees, or other objects in the flight area, handling of props during installation or removal from the aircraft, or simply from bouncing around in the storage compartment of the drone case.

Most professional sUAS have maintenance recommendations of prop replacement every 20 hours/50 flights or similar. Absent this manufacturer recommendation, all props should be replaced in accordance with above recommendations. Immediately replace any chipped or damaged prop.

> **Propeller replacements are recommended after every 20 hours (~50 flights).**

It is recommended that a full replacement set plus two be carried on all operations. In the event of a tip-over on landing, Foreign-Object Damage (FOD), or mid-flight mishap, it's possible, even likely that more than two props will require replacement. Some aircraft tend to tip over on their side in light winds, typically chipping or splitting at least one propeller if not two (this can usually be avoided landing nose or tail straight into wind).

> **When launching and landing, keep the aircraft's nose (or tail) directly into relative wind to avoid tip-overs.**

Try to make a habit of launching and landing with nose (or tail) directly into relative wind (the direction the wind is coming from) for best launch and land experiences. This helps avoid challenging situations during launch/land, such as tip overs due to wind gusts.

Flying with damaged props is a specific violation of the FAA FARs part 91 and 107.

Carry plenty of spares.

FILTERS

It is virtually impossible to run a successful UAS operation without filters for the camera lens. Regardless of camera used, filters are necessary to cut down on excess light, particularly when large apertures such as the most common f2.8 are used. In situations where higher quality sensors and glass are available, filters are still required, simply to cut down on light with optimal, low framerates.

> **Filters are an essential accessory in any UAS production kit.**

low shutter speeds reduce the issue of "jello cam" or "rolling shutter" effect, necessary for professional video capture (Still images do not suffer from rolling shutter due to the sensor re-setting per image).

This type of filter snaps on top of the camera lens. Some filters thread-mount on the camera similar to how filters mount on DSLR camera lenses. **Filters are a requisite component of any UAS production kit.**

Most of the fixed-mount camera UAS are fixed aperture. As the industry experiences technical advances, more camera systems will likely be developed with larger sensors and adjustable apertures. However, large sensors and adjustable

aperture systems will still require filters on the lens, particularly for video purposes. CMOS sensors, unless they are a
global shutter, will almost always induce artifacts and jello at
speeds higher than 1/250. Shutter speeds between 1/60 and
1/250 are highly desired.

> **Shutter speeds between 1/60 and 1/250 are highly desired for optimal footage.**

When shooting video, it's highly recommended to use a
shutter speed double the capture framerate. For example, a
recorded framerate of 30fps/30p would set a shutter speed
of 1/60. A recorded framerate of 50fps would do well with a
shutter speed of 1/100.

What Sort of Filters are Needed for UAS Work?

A set of Neutral Density/ND filters are most common in
a UAS workflow. A range of Neutral Density filters are
best.

ND8	Low light environments with direct sunlight, i.e.; sunrise/sunset hours
ND16	Bright sunny day, low/no clouds, outside of noon hours
ND32	Daylight/bright sunlight, clear skies, particularly around the noon hours
ND64	Best used for midday sun in desert, water, or snow environments. Also used in extremely bright sunlight over lightly-colored concrete

Polarizing filters are very useful for general use; these are great for reducing/eliminating glare. Polarizers are either circular or linear; both will work well for UAS; if using a circular polarizer (CP), be certain the polarizing lines are lined up horizontally, or rotated to the proper angle to reduce glare to the desired point.

UV Filters are also used for UAS work; these are only useful as lens protection. UV filters are good for haze reduction and smog, yet digital sensors are not sensitive to haze in the manner a film camera is sensitive. A polarizer plus post processing in tools such as Adobe LightRoom®, Photoshop®, ACDsee®, Skylum/Luminar, or other photo editing tool will generally provide sufficient power to reduce haze.

Tools are available in most photo or video editing tools for haze reduction/ elimination. The "Dehaze" filter found in Adobe video editing applications is fast and intuitive.

Lighting

Night UAS Flight

If flight at night is part of the mission requirement, lighting will be a requirement as per FAA requirement. More information related to night flight may be found in A Pilot's Manual to UAS Night Flight. At the time of this writing, there is no sUAS system with built-in lighting that meets the FAA requirement of three-mile visibility-capable lights that strobe at the required 40 cycles per minute (minimum) to 100 cycles per minute (maximum).

Per FAR § 23.1401 Anti-collision light system.

a. *General. The airplane must have an anti-collision light system that:*

  1. *Consists of one or more approved anti-collision lights located so that their light will not impair the flight crewmembers' vision or detract from the conspicuity of the position lights; and*

  2. *Meets the requirements of paragraphs (b) through (f) of this section.*

  b. ***Field of coverage.*** *The system must consist of enough lights to illuminate the vital areas around the airplane, considering the physical configuration and flight characteristics of the airplane. The field of coverage must extend in each direction within at least 75 degrees above and 75 degrees below the horizontal plane of the airplane, except that there may be solid angles of obstructed visibility totaling not more than 0.5 steradians.*

  c. ***Flashing characteristics.*** *The arrangement of the system, that is, the number of light sources,*

> *beam width, speed of rotation, and other characteristics, must give an effective flash frequency of **not less than 40, nor more than 100, cycles per minute.** The effective flash frequency is the frequency at which the airplane's complete anti-collision light system is observed from a distance and applies to each sector of light including any overlaps that exist when the system consists of more than one light source. In overlaps, flash frequencies may exceed 100, but not 180, cycles per minute.*
>
> d. **Color.** *Each anti-collision light must be either aviation red or aviation white and must meet the applicable requirements of § 23.1397.*

There are additional requirements, predominantly related to Part 61 (Manned) aircraft operations, and therefore not listed in this book.

> Commercial UAV flights, at night, require a "Night waiver" from the FAA.

Commercial flight at night requires an FAA waiver for Part 107.29. Learn more about training, applying for/receiving a waiver, and executing night-time missions before attempting a night flight. The A Pilot's Manual to UAS Night Flight is a great starting point.

Other Lighting Uses

Lighting isn't exclusively for night flight; lighting is of benefit during roofing inspections, lighting up areas under eaves, reducing shadows in early morning or late afternoon flights.

It is important to be aware: adding lighting to the aircraft provides additional weight to the aircraft. It is important that lights are mounted securely and properly mounted for optimal center of gravity/CG. Mounted lights may provide additional stability and controllability to some sUAS systems. Aircraft lights may also be used as ground lighting to backlight or highlight key elements of a property, adding value to the aircraft flight.

FoxFury Rugo lights may be mounted on virtually any sort of aircraft system. Waterproof and virtually indestructible, these lights offer a flood-light, spot light, or flat light source, providing tremendous versatility with three intensity settings. These lights strobe at a fixed rate.

Lumecube are another common instrument for action photographers and are ideal for UAS use. These small lights are waterproof with 10 levels of intensity and may be mounted on virtually any UAS system. These lights do strobe and may be controlled (short range) via Bluetooth on Android or iOS devices.

Although this is fully lit with daylight, the shadows may hide the underside. Using bright lighting, even in daylight, can reduce shadows and offer better image information.

In this brightly side-lit image, small lighting instruments such as the Lume-cube or FoxFury Rugo provide just enough light to balance the darker, naturally unlit areas, thus creating a more detailed image.

> **Avoid "tape-on" types of lighting for the aircraft.**

We do recommend avoiding the "tape-on" types of lighting available on low-budget websites. These devices are rarely reliable, and rarely meet FAA requirements for distance, intensity, color, and strobe cycle.

An advantage of self-powered lighting instruments such as the FoxFury or Lumecube instruments is that in the event of an incident at night, the aircraft may easily be located. Although most UAS crashes lead to battery/power separation resulting in no power to light the crashed aircraft. Self-powered lighting is separate from the aircraft and will remain lit in virtually any scenario.

PLANNING THE FLIGHT

UAV flight is 90% planning and post-production and 10% flying....

— Douglas Spotted Eagle

Planning the flight is requisite regardless of the client or customer. Without a plan, even experienced pilots arrive on site with a "**Ready, Fire, Aim**" mindset. We've come across "professionals" that show up on a shoot/project with the "*shoot everything and find the good stuff later*" mindset. This doesn't work very well in most instances and is remarkably inefficient.

Professionals will not only plan flights in advance but will develop a set of shots that will become repetitive and "cookie-cutter" in strategy and style, saving time, and providing a series of options to the property owner.

> Jack of all trades, master of none. Seek to round out skills that you are not core to your background.

Any camera operator has a series of practiced movements and angles in their repertoire; this is what sets good camera operators apart from great camera operators. Where the topic of UAS becomes interesting is the pilot's skills and abilities with either the camera or the aircraft. There are many pilots in the world that came to the flying UAS as expert photographers, yet they're not expert, nor even average pilots (yet). On the other hand, there are UAS pilots who fly exceptionally well, but are not photographers and know little about photography, frame rates, f-stops, filters, rule of thirds, and best angles for emotional and intellectual impact. Still yet are the rare few that have put the extra time into their own weaknesses and developed the complementary skills that bring their ability to a balance and continue to fly and shoot to improve their skillset. Flying techniques (for video) are presented in later sections of this book.

PLANNING POINTS

When a flight is proceeding incredibly well, something was forgotten.

— Robert Livingston

Being aware of basic requirements will help pre-plan the flight and guide conversations with clients, be they homeowners, real estate agencies, or photographer responsible for inside image/video capture.

With these thoughts in mind, plan on asking questions or offering recommendations to the client and related parties.

Time of Operation (Morning, Afternoon, Dusk, or Night)

The time of operation plays a role in the planning process. Take great effort to shoot any property with the sun at the front of operation (at pilot's/camera's back). This may impact decisions regarding Visual Observer participation, waiver application (night flight), and lighting (sunrise/sunset).

In this image, the time of day/sun light creates extreme angles that are not flattering to the home. Additionally, the photographer/pilot's shadow is visible in the image.

"Staging" For the Shot

Any qualified real estate agent knows how to stage a yard for ground level view. Many real estate agents will have no idea of staging a home for a UAS shoot. There will be times where there is no real estate agent involved and the seller will need coaching. Recommend that the home-owner hire someone who specializes in staging. Avoid being their "coach" for many reasons, the first of which is to avoid any claim of responsibility if the home doesn't sell. Meet with the staging agent and let them know what may be unique with aerial photo or video. Staging for an overhead shoot is only slightly different, yet those differences may be very significant.

Explain to the real estate agent, home-owner, or staging professional that the yard/house must be staged prior to arrival of the flight crew. Time is money, and the flight crew isn't paid for sitting around watching others stage the yard or home exterior.

Staging Points

Roof valleys:

Clear leaves, needles, or other debris from valleys/areas between roof pitches. These can be professionally

cleaned, or homeowners can use a gas-powered leaf blower (never use electric blowers with extension cables that might trip the operator).

Gutters:

Clear gutters of debris such as leaves, needles, algae, Frisbee's, baseballs, or anything else that may be in the gutter.

Mossy/Algae roof

There are many cleaning agents that may be used to clean moss or algae off the roof. Never use chlorine or similar agents that will kill grass on the ground.

Remove holiday lighting from rooflines (and other areas around the home)

Holiday lighting is distracting, breaks up clean lines, and either dates the image or generally suggests the home hasn't been well cared-for.

> **Prospective homebuyers can look through photos or videos and mentally add their own possessions, but they cannot subtract things as easily. Less is more.**

Backlighting dark areas against the home/foliage:

Small lighting devices can make a difference in the way that the walls of a home. Tools like the FoxFury Rugo or Lume-cube lighting instruments are invaluable. LitePanels also offer battery-powered lighting instruments that are very small and may be hidden in foliage. This sort of lighting is most effective in early morning or late afternoon shoots.

Hide Trashcans

Trashcans can be put inside a garage or outbuilding; they detract from any image. (And be sure to know which day is "garbage day" to avoid shooting footage on the schedule trash pickup day.

Access points

Close all doors, windows, including the garage door.

Basic Expectations (Residential)

There are references to flying techniques in the following paragraphs. These flying techniques are addressed by name, in other sections of this book.

Address

- Capture the address of the home. There are usually at least one of three angles from which this may be captured.
  - House number painted on the curb (excellent opportunity for rotate reveal technique)
  - House number on the mail box (Pull reveals work well in this instance, as do strafes)
  - House number on front of home (Push or pull reveals work well for these sorts of shots, strafes will sometimes work well.

Lead down street to home

- "Drive" the prospective homeowner down the street to the open house/home for sale
  - Gods-Eye, push reveal, or hook shot are useful techniques for this stock shot.

Front of home @ 45 angle

- For both photos and video, it's a good idea to capture a safety angle that can be used for stills, and for editing between other video techniques. This shows the front of home, yard, driveway, etc.

Top down/90

- This is the Gods-Eye view, both for photo and video. Camera angled straight down at an altitude high enough to capture the majority of the property

boundaries. Capture safety stills and video for mid-point editing or transitional editing points.

Back of home @45

- For both photos and video, it's a good idea to capture a safety angle that can be used for stills, and for editing between other video techniques. This shows the back of home, yard, playground, pool, outbuildings, etc.

POI of home

- Capture all four sides of the home for purposes of photo and video mid-point edits. These sorts of shot angles are good go-to angles in the event of necessary edit transition points. This angle may also be accomplished through a simple orbit at a static altitude.

High altitude: Neighborhood rotation or feature towards parks, shopping centers, etc.

- Demonstrate the neighborhood from a higher altitude. A Hook/J shot is excellent for this sort of angle, as it allows the home to be half-orbited while climbing in altitude.

Capturing all these angles and features on every shoot will ensure that all content necessary for a quality edit will be available in the editing stage of any production, and they take very little time to capture.

Additional shots, time permitting, or edit-requiring will also aid in the editing stage. These sorts of shots are dependent on other content being cut into any video presentation.

Additional Shot Examples:

Fly up to door/back from front door

- This shot is extremely useful when transitioning to inside video, providing an edit point to inside the home. If the home is overhung or has an enclosed portico, fly a pull reveal and reverse the flight in post, creating the appearance of the UAS flying toward the home.

Flight up/down driveway path

- A Hook/J shot is valuable here, as it may demonstrate the length or quality of the driveway that begins or finishes in a half-orbit of the property.

Orbit around home

- In our view, this shot should always be included in any production. For purposes of a general file for websites that only allow short videos (some only allow five-second video) or for cutting into/out of other shots/angles, orbits are not only a feature technique, but also a safety technique.

Basic Expectations (Commercial)

Address

- Capture the address of the business
  - ○ Capture the building directory if outdoors
  - ○ Capture any marquee signage on the awnings of the building
  - ○ Capture the monument sign at the driveway entrance to the building
  - ○ Capture any pylon signage directing traffic/visitors/shipping around the building

Lead down street to business/office space

- "Drive" the prospective homeowner down the street to the business/office space
  - ○ Gods-Eye, push reveal, or hook shot are useful techniques for this stock shot

Front of business/office @ 45 angle

- For both photos and video, it's a good idea to capture a safety angle that can be used for stills, and for editing between other video techniques. This shows the front of business, parking log, mailboxes, awning/entrances, lobby features, etc.

Top down/90

- This is the Gods-Eye view, both for photo and video. Camera angled straight down at an altitude high enough to capture the majority of the property boundaries. Capture safety stills and video for mid-point editing or transitional editing points

Back of business @45

- For both photos and video, it's a good idea to capture a safety angle that can be used for stills, and for editing between other video techniques. This shows the back of business, parking lot, employee areas, shared spaces, refuse/trash areas, outbuildings, shipping areas, etc.

Highlight value-add space

- Capture any areas or traffic routing that offers ease of access for shipping vehicles, loading docks, multi-level parking areas

"Climb the building" with vertical shots of the top to bottom or bottom to top of the building.

- This is particularly effective on buildings greater than three stories in height. The climb may become an area or outbuilding reveal. This same technique may be valuable for a parking structure

POI of business

- Capture all four sides of the business for purposes of photo and video mid-point edits. These sorts of shot angles are good go-to angles in the event of necessary edit transition points. This angle may also be accomplished through a simple orbit at a static altitude

High altitude: Neighborhood rotation or feature towards parks, shopping centers, etc.

- Demonstrate the neighborhood from a higher altitude. A Hook/J shot is excellent for this sort of angle, as it allows the building or office space to be half-orbited while climbing in altitude

Capturing all these angles and features on every shoot will ensure that all content necessary for a quality edit will be available in the editing stage of any production, and they take very little time to capture.

Try to find a time when the parking lot is empty. If such a time cannot be located, plan on spending time in the video or photo editor to remove/obscure license plates.

Things to Avoid While Shooting Residential Real Estate

There are things to avoid when shooting any residence in a neighborhood. Although these issues may seem like they're common sense (common sense frequently isn't common), avoiding these things in the neighborhood may keep the pilot or the real estate agent out of hot water.

For example:

People:

Explain to the homeowner that if they wish to be home, that they don't come outside. Ask the homeowner to notify guests, neighbors, and family members that an aerial shoot is occurring between the hours of XX and XX on XX date, and that their non-presence will be appreciated.

Pets:

Spinning blades and pets don't mix, so this is the first point of UAS and pets. Additionally, pets in a yard will be bothered by the presence of the UAS and will often wildly run around in the yard or runs. This does not make for attractive video or photos.

Other addresses:

Avoid capturing other home addresses in the video or stills. If this is unavoidable, use a blurring tool or pixilation tool in the video or photo editing application.

License plates:

Advise homeowners to remove cars from driveways or from parking in front of the house. If a neighbor's car is parked within the area to be captured. Ensure the production vehicles are not parked within view. In the event that license plate capture is unavoidable, use a blur or pixilation tool to obfuscate a visible license plate.

Children:

Ensure that parents understand the activity in the area may incidentally capture children.

> **Bottom line: Keep the property as tidy and clean as possible for its photo shoot for best end results.**

Manual or Automated Flight?

Different properties may require different flight techniques. If the property owner requests orthomaps, automated flight will be called for. If the property owner requests 3D modeling, automated flight is called for.

If the property is in a wide-open space, either automation or manual flight may apply.

Perhaps the property owner or real estate agent would like a flight plan or pre-flight experience in Google Earth or other application, with the pre-flight to be transferred to the UAS.

These are just a few examples of where automation over manual may be a consideration.

Manual flight offers rapid access to a finished product where automation may be a bit slower in the pre-plan, yet the outcome is guaranteed, barring any environmental issue.

> **Keep it Short, Simple, Specific. The KISS principle helps drive speed to delivery.**

One of the benefits of manual flight is that the pilot and crew can apply "cookie cutter" techniques for very fast editing and post-processing. Automation will generally vary from location to location. Creating a workflow that will be most efficient in post-processing and video editing will provide the best path to profitability. The KISSS (Keep It Short, Simple, Specific) principle absolutely applies. Speed to edit means speed to delivery, and speedy delivery is the end-game goal.

Notifying Neighbors or HOA

Privacy is of significant concern in many neighborhoods, and there are home-owner associations that have generated no-fly policies in the neighborhood. These sorts of neighbor-hoods may be challenging, and be prepared for lead time prior to the flight, to achieve local permissions to fly. As time goes on, it seems these local/community restrictions will be relaxed. Approach to the HOA should be managed by the real estate agent and HOA representative.

Regardless of the location and any restrictions, it is best to notify neighbors and those who may be entering the neigh-borhood that active UAS flight is occurring. This may be done via multiple methods.

- Flyers in mailboxes 48-72 hours in advance, notifying neighbors of active UAS operations on XX day and XX time. Be sure to mention that no images will be captured of uninvolved homes, and include a phone number or email for questions

- Sandwich board in neighborhood, placed 24 hours in advance
- Door to door notification (this is efficient only in small neighborhoods or areas with large lots)

Notification in advance will reduce tension and stress, questions and interruptions from concerned and uninformed neighbors. Even in small operations, this is where a second team member is valuable, to take questions, act as a visual observer, and prevent any interruptions to the pilot and flight operations.

Notify Law Enforcement

Informing local police that active flight operations will be occurring at a particular location at a specific time, may prevent the police from showing up at the location due to a phone call from a neighbor that missed the notifications. Unless there is a community ordinance preventing flight from community property, the only conversation with law enforcement is the notification. Out of courtesy, we recommend law enforcement be notified shortly prior to launch and notified when flight operations are complete.

Filing A NOTAM (Notice To Airmen)

NOTAMS are a means of notifying Air Traffic Control and pilots that UAS operations are occurring in a specific area. A NOTAM is *not* permission to fly. A NOTAM is merely a notification that operations will occur in the area. A NOTAM does not prevent others from flying in the area in which UAS operations are occurring. It does not lock down the airspace so that no one else is able to fly through that airspace/area. It serves as a warning. Regardless of a NOTAM, manned aircraft always have right-of-way, and UAS must provide that right of way at all times (Refer to FAR 107.23, 107.37, 107. 43, and 91.13 as a secondary issue).

Filing a NOTAM is not required. It is advisable, however, particularly in high-traffic areas. It's a good practice and may be valuable in the event of an incident or questionable operation.

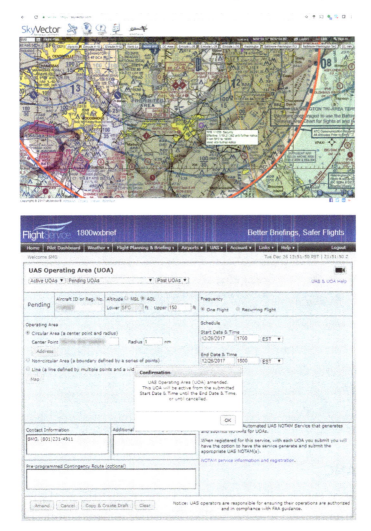

Filing The NOTAM:

- Browse to 1800wxbrief.com
- Create an account
- Select UAS from the menu bar
- Fill out the application form, all fields required
- Choose "Submit".
- The system will notify that the NOTAM has been filed.

Verify the NOTAM has been filed by browsing to www. skyvector.com

Navigate to the area of flight operations, and in the "Layers" menu, ensure that "DROTAMS" is checked.

The Drone **NOTAM (DROTAM)** should be indicated with a purple outline, and pop-up information indicating time operation begins/ends, and date.

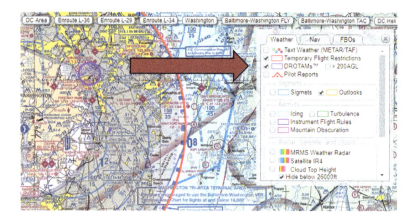

LAANC

Persons reading this book are either already RPC pilots, or will soon challenge the FAA RPC/Part 107 examination. Those persons should know about the Low Altitude Authorization and Notification Capability (LAANC) System.

The FAA has authorized flight services in controlled airspace through (at the time of this writing) three software application development and services providers.

- AirMap
- Project Wing
- Skyward

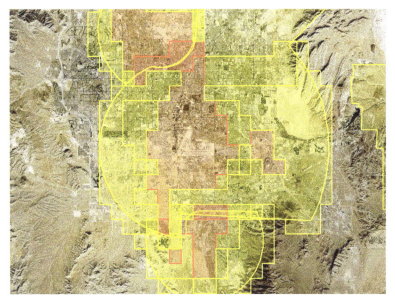

An overall view of Las Vegas, NV and the high-view of the LAANC system

These services enable RPC pilots access to low altitude authorizations in Bravo, Charlie, Delta, and Echo airspace. These are a means of rapid authorizations in most areas. There are some airports and regions not in the LAANC system yet; the FAA is rapidly adding authorized areas.

Closeup view of the Las Vegas, NV LAANC

Notifying ATC

All efforts are being made by the FAA to reduce/remove contact with the Air Traffic Control (ATC) to reduce the load on existing services. However, there will be instances that ATC notification is required. Be familiar with the language of any existing waivers and make all attempts to remain familiar with FAA requirements, updates, and changes in the system.

> **Stay abreast of FAA changes/updates by visiting www.faadronezone.faa.gov**

FLYING TECHNIQUES

There's simply no substitute for experience in terms of aviation safety.

— Chesley "Sully" Sullenberger

Practice builds experience, and experience breeds many emotions, opportunities, and understandings.

Practicing the video moves suggested in this section will ensure the client will be happy. They're broken down into "fundamental" video skills, "nice to have" video skills, and "advanced" video skills. Plan on at least 40 hours of flight (approximately 90 flights) to be competent in the "fundamental" skills category. Practice each move for at least five

> **40 hours of flight (~90 flights) brings competency on "fundamental skills".**

battery changeouts before moving on to the next challenge/skill. Master each of the fundamental skills prior to moving on to the next set.

Fundamental Skills

Hover/Hover Reveal

Hovering is not as easy as one might think. Several types of GPS systems allow a UAS to stay fairly well on station; adding a yaw to the hover becomes much more difficult to maintain the vertical position of the hover. This relatively simple shot is extremely effective and dramatic when there is a pool, fountain, or other high-value, small area feature. Imagine a shot where the entire frame is filled with beautiful blue as the UAS climbs, camera rotating, and a beautiful pool and hot tub are revealed. This is a one-stick technique with the camera pointing straight down and is a very powerful introduction technique to introduce a property, particularly if the roof is unusual in design or material. If the camera can be separately yawed, the left stick is at the top of the stickwell, while the camera is rotated with the camera yaw control. If the camera cannot be yawed, the stick is pointed to the 10 o'clock or 2 o'clock position.

God's Eye Following A Path

The "God's-eye" following a path skill is ideal for leading viewers down a street to a home, overflying a yard, a general overview of driving directions in a given area, and more. This tech-

nique is essentially a hover with forward motion. It is also a basic technique on which other skills may be built and developed into a "style" repertoire. The aircraft is typically flown slowly but can be flown quickly with a smooth control. This single-stick technique does not use the gimbal control on the GSC.

The aircraft is primarily steered using the right stick. However, curves in a path or road may be accommodated through using the left stick to yaw the aircraft in the direction of the curve.

Aircraft that have a camera adjustment may be used instead of the yaw.

Push Reveal

The Push Reveal is identical to a cinematic move where the camera is on a dolly pushing forward, and frequently rising

in altitude. This technique is ideal for big reveals of a home behind a brick wall or fence, trees, or other obstacles.

The aircraft is pushed/flown forward at a reasonably low altitude. Pilots should take note that the aircraft will be nose-down and will lose altitude over distance. This runs the risk of flying into the ground. This is referred to as a CFIT (pronounced "Cee-Fit) or "controlled flight into terrain." Keep the left stick slightly up while driving forward, and upon approaching the subject (building or feature), climb in altitude, typically very quickly. This will reveal the subject and can be very dramatic. This is also a basic shot style on which other styles may be built. This single-stick technique does not use the gimbal control on the GSC.

> The "Push Reveal" is a "trucking" shot where the aircraft flies forward level and then upward, revealing a subject behind the first-seen subject.

Pull Reveal

A Pull-Reveal is an extremely powerful technique that allows the viewer to see a close-up of a feature on a home or building, with the UAS flying backward to reveal the bigger picture/entire building or subject. The key to a solid pull reveal is to keep even pressure on the stick as the aircraft pulls away, with no pressure variance on the stick. This is a single-stick technique that does not use the gimbal control on the GSC. Adding a lift in altitude during the pull is also an effective technique that will not only reveal the subject/home, but also reveal the area where the subject/home is located.

> The "Pull Reveal" showcases up-close views first, pulling back to reveal the entire area.

Static Tilt

With the aircraft hovering in one place, use the tilt/pitch control to shift the pitch (angle) of the camera view. While this shot is usually a top-downward movement, it may be equally powerful when pitching up as well.

Strafe

The strafe is simply a side slide. The camera/nose of the aircraft are oriented towards the subject while the right stick is used to slide the aircraft past the subject/building. The key

to a solid strafe is to begin the strafe well before the building comes into the camera frame and continue static speed until well after the object of interest has exited the camera frame. This is a single stick technique and does not use the gimbal control of the GSC.

Be certain the aircraft is at full speed well before the "start record" point (although the camera should be rolling at all times).

Panning Shot

A panning shot should be very easy to achieve, yet there is difficulty in the timing. Pans are a hover with a horizontal rotation/yaw. The aircraft may be yawed, or the camera may be yawed. Practice this technique  with a horizontal object (such as a roofline) to determine if altitude is being lost during the yaw. Some UAS dashboards offer a Rule of Thirds line overlay to help identify situations where the UAS is sinking or rising (sinking altitude is common in early panning/yaw during hover).

The most difficult aspect of a clean panning shot is to begin the pan by ramping the rotation well before the object being panned comes into frame,  maintaining a constant speed across the pan, and ramping speed down to the hover. Particularly when shooting slow framerates such as 24p, practice the pan, and watch the pan on a monitor after a few practice pans have been achieved. Pacing is critical to a successful pan, particularly when there are windows or other objects that break up the texture/surface of the object being filmed. *Slow is smooth, smooth is fast* in learning the cadence of a solid pan.

Slow is smooth, smooth is fast. Learn these techniques while moving slowly. Speed will come with muscle memory, with muscle memory comes confidence and competence.

> **Remember: Slow is smooth; Smooth is fast. Don't rush the pan shot; Doing the shot slowly offers more flexibility in post.**

Half-Orbit

Half-orbits are likely the most difficult basic flight technique to learn. Rather than flying a straight line like a strafe, the aircraft is in a semi-circle while the camera remains pointed at the home/building/subject. To achieve this technique, the right stick is pushed slightly to the right or left, and the

left stick is pushed slightly to the left or right (sticks are always opposite from each other for this technique). The half-orbit is a fundamental technique on which other axis and movements can be built for very dramatic footage. The technique is a combination of a yaw and side slide/strafe. This two-stick technique does not use the gimbal control of the GSC.

"Nice to Have" Skills

These skills are not difficult once the fundamentals are mastered. They are "add-ons" to previously learned skills.

Again, these skills require additional practice to master both in technique and muscle memory.

Rotate Reveal

A Rotate Reveal is a technique that begins the flight with the camera focused on one object/feature and rotates to the main feature while climbing in altitude.

Launch the UAS pointing towards a secondary feature. For example, perhaps a residential yard ornament or name placard in front of a business will be the beginning point. As the UAS launches/climbs in altitude using the left stick, the UAS is rotated (yawed) by rotating the left stick to the 9 o'clock position. The main feature/building is then revealed, visually tied to the yard ornament or the name placard. If the aircraft has a gimbal capable of yaw, this is best achieved via gimbal vs yawing the aircraft.

> This more challenging flight skill can be quite powerful in final edits. Mastering it takes practice.

Pull Reveal with Gimbal Movement

Recalling the technique of the pull reveal, the flight begins with the camera pointing downward, perhaps as much as 90 degrees down, depending on the situation. The UAS will fly backward, nose facing the object/building. As the UAS flies backward, slowly raise the altitude and pull up the camera to full view of the building or object. The most challenging component of this technique is the left stick rising up while the right stick is down while simultaneously moving the camera controls. Adding camera or aircraft yaw post-reveal can be very powerful.

Advanced Skills

Hook Shot

This is also known as a "J-Shot" or "Flying a J." The aircraft flies a half-orbit, ending with a strafe. During the strafe, the camera continues to

145

focus on the previously orbited object/home. This is a particularly valuable technique in commercial real estate flight, as it can show the size of a building in relationship to its surrounding area, in addition to showing the location with the building in it. Of course, the area surrounding the building can be shown through several sorts of shooting techniques yet the "Hook Shot/J" allows dynamic motion to build the tension into the shot as the strafe pulls away from the location. This is a very easy technique for a two-operator team, yet only marginally difficult for a single operator. Practice will make this an easy shot. A UAV with a rotation/yaw-capable camera will be much more efficient and clean in this particular technique. The Hook/J shot can also be flown toward the object and hook around the object once the object is aligned with the half-orbit distance. This technique requires two sticks and potentially a camera yaw control, dependent on the UAS being flown.

Full Orbit

A full orbit is a nose-in rotation where the camera stays focused on the object all the way around. This is an effective technique for  showing any tall building, feature, tower, or other tall/vertical object. This two-stick technique is achievable through automation yet being able to manually control the aircraft demonstrates a greater emotion, or power. This technique can be dramatically improved by adding a corkscrew where the aircraft is climbing (or descending) in altitude while fully orbiting a feature. Orbiting the feature more than once is very powerful while climbing. With sticks at opposite sides of the GSC facing in opposite directions, this technique can be very quick to learn, yet far more difficult to master.

Nose-Out Full Orbit

Being able to fly a full orbit is a valuable technique in the tool box. Reversing the orbit to a nose-out orbit is a bit more difficult, simply because the center  point of the object cannot be seen with the camera. The tail of the aircraft points toward the object being orbited, while the camera provides a circular view of the area surrounding the building. A valuable technique, particularly when edited next to/in sequence with a nose-in orbit, this technique can show a spectacular view of the area surrounding a tall building.

This is more easily achieved with a camera system that offers a Point of Interest feature, where the camera is always pointing at the object. However, using "preset" camera moves may impact the pilot's skills, and reduce the number of movements available during the mission.

Oblong Orbit

An oblong orbit is as its name implies; a non-rounded orbit. The technique is challenging not in the orbit, but in the shift from the orbit to the straight/strafe points. In flying scenarios where a building or feature is longer than wide, this is a very useful technique. Essentially, the oblong orbit is two half orbits connected to two strafe runs. This can also be easily converted to an egg-shaped orbit by angling the strafes into a much smaller half-orbit at one end of the oblong travel.

The most important aspect of these shots on any property, is that the cadence/speed of movement remains consistent throughout. It is nearly impossible to cut fast moving video into slow-moving video when capturing real estate content. Consistency is key. One technique is to play music either through a headphone (one ear, so the pilot can hear what's happening around them) or have a song playing in the back of the pilot's mind. The rhythm of a song will help the pilot maintain a consistent speed. Looking at the airspeed indicator will also help, but once it's realized the UAS has been flying faster or slower, requires a re-do of the shot. Timing is very difficult to repair in post; get it right in the field. With practice, timing becomes second nature.

INDOOR SHOOTING TECHNIQUES

Hand-held gimbals, and even hand-held UAS acting as a gimbal, may be used to capture or introduce the inside areas of a residence or commercial building. Prior to the advent of hand-held gimbals, professional pilots would often walk the inside of a residence or commercial building while hand-holding the UAS with careful steps and slow movement, keeping an interior fluidity consistent with images captured in flight.

When shooting indoors, keep the camera clear of walls, and centered to the middle of hallways, doors, rooms, and any objects in the room such as kitchen islands, bars, etc. If the camera is close to walls or obstacles, perspective becomes distorted and while perhaps very artistic, home and business building buyers are not looking for art, they are looking for accurate, distortion-free images of the room.

Carry the camera (or UAS) at waist level. This provides a standard view throughout the building/residence and allows viewers to have a reasonably accurate view from a unique angle that is generally flattering to most sorts of rooms. It also is less physically taxing.

Another creative shot angle is to stand on a stepstool or short ladder near ceiling height, with the camera at a 45°

downward angle. Slowly pan the room, matching the pan cadence of any outdoor flight. We recommend that pans left to right, and right to left be captured for editing choices. Generally, gimbaled movement is limited to walk-through, but if panning shots are captured, always capture pans in both directions to provide editing choices (if both directions are not captured, direction can always be manipulated in post-processing/editing stages).

If the building has a feature that can be 'orbited,' then do so. An example might be a large kitchen island, long bar, or perhaps an indoor fountain. Orbit the feature in the same style and cadence that an outdoor orbit would be achieved.

CREATING A STOCK SHOT LIST

Having a basketful of stock flight techniques won't carry enough creativity to satisfy the client. Having several angular techniques is necessary yet knowing what the angles will capture is equally important. A stock shot list is expected by most clients and real estate agencies. They will either specify standard shots or ask that the drone pilot provide a list/menu of shots.

When meeting with a client, having a selection of images on a tablet or photobook demonstrating these stock shots will aid in communicating the opportunity and their desire. Offer at least three versions of each stock shot in the list. This will assist the client in communicating with the producer or pilot and assist the team in planning the shoot in advance of the flight. Having a stock set of moves greatly speeds the editing process and allows the operation to be overall more efficient.

> Have a portfolio of aerial images to show new clients what they can expect. Not only does this assist in clearly communicating expectations between the client and pilot, it will also streamline the editing process for final product.

MAPPING IMAGES

Capturing images for mapping is a very different process from flying techniques to artistically and emotionally present a property. Mapping may be desired for a few reasons:

1. The client may want a larger two-dimensional example of the property that may be viewed in great depth and detail.

2. The client may desire a 3D rendering of the property.

3. The client may wish to add the larger map to a plat or Google Earth (or other mapping application) to illustrate change over time in a given geographic region.

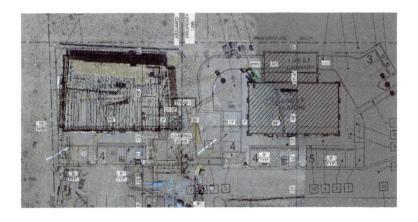

Mapping is achieved through taking many images of an area and stitching them together in a software application, to provide a flat, single image that contains great detail. Achieving maps is not quite as simple as flying in straight lines and taking photos, however.

Automation is by far the preferred method of mapping flight. Automation ensures photos are captured at specific, equal intervals over time or distance, and ensures precise overlapping, camera position, and no missed areas of capture. Tools such as DroneDeploy™, Pix4DCapture™, Yuneec DataPilot™, AutoDesk Recapture, Litchi, and similar applications enable automated flight for precision, speed, and quality of image data.

Not all UAS systems are capable of automated flight control. Manual flight may also be used for capturing image data for mapping, provided the pilot is methodical, paced, and patient. However, manual flight is costlier in terms of time, risk of error, battery life, and control. Practice will go a long way to ensuring all necessary data is captured.

Stitching applications use GPS/UTM coordinates to help place image location, altitude, speed/distance between captures, yet GPS data alone does not ensure quality image capture. The GPS coordinates, altitude, speed, and other data are found in the EXIF data file embedded in the JPEG metadata.

The highest quality imagery is found when using RAW/DNG photosets. Unfortunately, EXIF data is not found in RAW/DNG images. Some applications allow image placement using JPEG with EXIF as proxies to be replaced with the RAW/DNG images. Some UAS sensors allow both JPEG and RAW or DNG images to be captured simultaneously.

Regardless of whether flight is automated or manual capture, requirements are the same for data capture and input to a stitching or modelling application.

The first step is planning the flight. Flights are typically flown as "grids" where the UAS will fly "lawnmower" patterns. Automated flight programming will provide information regarding where batteries will require changing (if batteries will require changing mid-program), length of flight time, how many images will be taken, etc. This information assists the pilot in determining altitude, time of day for the flight, etc.

> **Automated flight is highly recommended for windy conditions, early morning/late evening when light is low to ensure critical details are captured cleanly.**

The "Nadir" image is the foundation for all mapping, whether two dimensional or three-dimensional.

Two-dimensional maps utilize images captured with the camera pointing straight down at the ground. This is referred to as "Nadir" angles. It is important the aircraft be capable of shooting straight down and capture a clear image. Clean images are determined by low/slow motion at the time of the shutter snap, and aircraft attitude. Ideally, the aircraft is flat in the air.

This oblique image will overlap the next image by 50%

If the aircraft is moving, or angles are off, it will be difficult for the stitching application to work with blurred or non-nadir images. Clear images are necessary for a clean map.

Just as clean nadir images are important, overlapping images are equally important. The greater the overlap, the greater the ability of the stitching application to stitch images together.

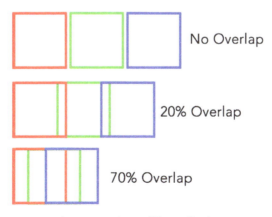

Image courtesy of DroneDeploy

Overlap will take a great toll on battery life and length of time in the flight and reduces the area the UAS can fly on each battery. However, overlap greatly increases the number of match points available to the stitching software, therefore reducing stitching artifacts.

Flight speed plays a critical role in capturing a stitch-quality image. High flight speed captures more images, yet greatly increases the risk of blurred images, and non-nadir flight. Slower flight also enables greater "Front-lap" imagery opportunity, again increasing total area coverage (TOC).

Ideally, a generally trustworthy recipe for mapping flights is:

- No faster than 12mph/17.6 ft/s
- 65% overlap/side-lap
- 35% front-lap (can be increased; there is a limit to how fast the camera can shoot. Once this limit is reached, there is no more front-lap value available)
- 100' altitude
- Daylight

Lower altitudes do offer greater resolution but require much slower flight. Resolutions are determined XX inch per pixel, and resolutions as low as one inch per-pixel are possible, provided the environment doesn't prevent the UAS from flying due to powerlines, telephone poles, trees, or other obstacles.

Some automation applications allow pilots to program a flight where the UAS stops at each image point, hovers, captures prior to moving to the next point. This method of flight is highly recommended in windy conditions, early morning/late evening when light is very low, or when criticality of detail is paramount. Hover/Capture techniques will shorten battery life by approximately 20%, yet usually provides much greater clarity in less than optimal conditions.

> Automated flight is highly recommended for windy conditions, early morning/late evening when light is low to ensure critical details are captured cleanly.

3D MODELLING

Modelling buildings in 3D can be accomplished via several different techniques that may vary dependent on software application recommendations. For example, one software application prefers nadir flight coupled with oblique (captured from the side) images. Other applications recommend orbiting an object/building at equal distances from the center of the building with multiple altitudes.

3D models will significantly improve through increasing both overlap/front-lap to 80%. This will generate greater flight time and number of images.

Another tip to improving 3D imagery is to fly on an overcast day or fly only at midday when shadows are minimized due to the angle of the sun.

Our recipe for 3D models is similar to what several software application developers recommend;

- Low-altitude orbit, camera angle at 30 degrees.
- High altitude orbit, camera angle at 45 degrees.
- Nadir orbit (or grid), camera angle at 0 degrees.

> Cameras with a mechanical or global shutter are superior to non-mechanical camera systems due to the lack of rolling shutter effect, commonly known as "jellocam." Reducing shutterspeed through use of filters will significantly benefit the 3D model process. Experiment with filters for best results when using electronic shutter-system UAS cameras (most UAS systems are electronic shutter).

If the grid/nadir/high altitude orbit is at 125' in altitude, the low altitude orbit will typically be half that altitude, depending on environment. Ultimately, a flight at 20' is ideal for capturing the average single story/split-level home, yet this ultimate height is rarely possible, simply due to trees, power poles, and other obstacles.

Creating ideal 3D models is different from location to location, environment to environment. Practice, practice, practice.

Image courtesy of Pix4D

Uniform Imagery

When there is little contrast or difference between photos, it is difficult for stitching applications to accurately layer images for a quality final image, free of artifacts. Stitching water, corn-fields/agriculture, parking lots, or any other area with highly repetitive features will be challenging. Capturing a home in the middle of a large section of agriculture and few/no additional differential features will be difficult to accurately stitch and nearly impossible to model.

If this sort of imagery is required, Ground Reference Points/Ground Control Point (GRP/GCP) or RTK GPS systems may be of value. Using RTK or GRP goes beyond the scope of this book, and we recommend that more specific research be undertaken if this is a requirement of a real estate project.

This is an example of a Ground Control Point (Courtesy DroneDeploy)

DELIVERY

> *Perfection has to do with the end product, but excellence has to do with the process.*
>
> *~Jerry Moran*

Three components are required for a successful delivery; A pilot capable of flying all necessary angles and techniques, quality image capture, and software to assemble the data into its finished form. There are many software tools available for every kind of image output. We'll examine some of the available tools in this section, ranging from free to paid-for subscriptions.

As high-speed turnaround is a critical component of the UAS-for-Real Estate workflow, we recommend that every organization develop techniques for file management that will aid in transferring, editing, delivering, and archiving footage.

Start with hard drives/HDD's by numbering the primary drive and its partnered backup drive. Our process is one folder per month, with a subfolder for every project. These are backed up at the end of each day. ALWAYS BACK UP FILES.

> When it comes to data storage, adopt the rule of "Two is one, and one is none." A backup ensures the client's data is safe in any event. If anything occurs to the original/primary drive, the backup may be used to create another copy.

Rename files on transfer. Files will come off the UAS with device/brand specific names. We recommend adopting a file structure/naming convention that will better describe the file. For example, a file may be camera-named **"YUN000132."** Renaming the file to **"Clark_Agency_121917_ YUN000132"** immediately provides name-searchable data by client name, date of flight, and original file name.

Delete bad photos and footage. UAS capture huge amounts of data yet there is no point in keeping the unusable data, and this ensures the bad data is never seen. Reduce storage where possible.

Manage files from a central point. One method of editing is to copy files to an "in-progress" storage device for purposes of editing. This means that three copies are created during the transfer process. Once editing is complete, remove the in-progress files from the "in-progress" drive. If the project is one that will be returned to over a long period of time, link files in the project to the respective drive where the original file transfer was stored.

> **Cull the raw data collected to reduce overall storage whenever possible. Don't keep anything that cannot be used in a final product.**

Image Processing (Photo)

Still Image Processing

 Photos often need to be corrected for lighting, color, or vignetting. If one image has issues, all images captured in the flight will likely have the same issues. Having a photo editor or processing application capable of "batch processing" images (Processing all images with the same settings in one pass, ensuring all images are identically corrected) is of significant benefit.

There are times where single images will need processing as well. Common changes in images are adjustment to saturation, contrast, haze reduction, cropping, and perhaps some minor adjustments to specific portions of images where reflections in windows, shadows on concrete or sides of houses, etc. need to be reduced.

There are several tools which are efficient and capable.

- Adobe Lightroom (Very powerful Photo-editing with batch processing)
- Adobe Photoshop (Very powerful Photo-editing with batch processing)
- ACDSee (Very powerful Photo-editing with batch processing)
- DXOpticsPro (Very powerful Photo-editing with batch processing)
- Corel Aftershot (Very powerful Photo-editing with batch processing)

- Luminar/Skylum (Intuitive, powerful, low-cost. By far the best batch editing tool we're aware of!)
- AffinityPhoto (Very powerful Photo-editing with batch processing, rapid selection/repair features)

3D/2D MAPPING TOOLS

Beyond capturing still images and video images, UAS are often used to create 2D or 3D maps of a property or a surrounding area. Due to the way these maps are made, the map detail is spectacular, and viewers may zoom in quite deeply to see specifics about the property.

Tools range in price and quality.

Tools exist which can rapidly assemble highly-detailed 2D photographs that are quite large, that may be color corrected after assembly. These 2D maps are referred to as "Orthmaps." The maps correct for the image curve most camera lenses generate, referred to as "ortho-rectifying" the image so that scale and edges are uniform, thus generating a map-accurate image. These images may be scaled and laid over printed or digital maps.

2D maps are very effective for showing a non-distorted, high resolution view of an area around a building. Of course, many other tools are available for "orthomapping."

Orthomapping tools may be found online or as localized tools ranging in cost from free to high-cost subscriptions.

> The advantage of using 3D information on a property allows buyers to better visualize the building(s) and surrounding areas. But a word of caution: determine the cost (time) vs. reward of generating a 3D map vs. a 2D map. (i.e. is it necessary?) Creating a 3D map requires a lot more processing time.

Detail in 3D maps can be very clean, allowing for reasonably accurate measurements by any stakeholder.

Choosing an Online Site (Cloud) vs. Local Rendering

Sites such as mapsmadeeasy.com, or opendronemap.org are not difficult to use, and for users that have high-speed internet and slow computers may want to use the online option. However, images from UAS can be quite large, and may require considerable time/bandwidth to upload images from a large area. The benefit of online systems is that the images are rendered in the background, freeing up cycles from the local computer. Once the final image is rendered, users can either download the rendered image or provide embeddable links to the client.

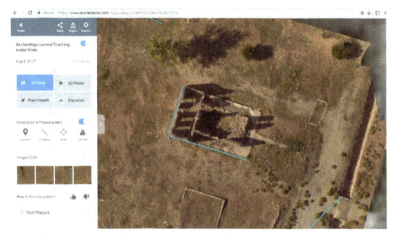

DroneDeploy is an online mapping application that frees up the host computer from intensive image processing.

Many of the tools capable of 2D images can generate 3D images; computer horsepower is the greatest difference in requirements. Tools such as Agisoft, Datumate, Bentley, Pix4D, DroneDeploy will all require significant processing power if files are to be locally rendered.

Pix4D is an online or desktop application that allows users to create 2D or 3D imaging.

VIDEO EDITING

 Video editing can be a tedious process, particularly if the shooting process was not disciplined and well-planned. Properly planned projects with a pre-conceived/pre-planned shooting order will significantly shorten the length of time required for editing.

> **Planning for the end product before editing starts will save a lot of time in the long run. Build the project library first!**

One of the longest and most arduous processes in editing is assembling the project library. Assets such as stock music (approved by client), stock graphics (transparent images of the agency logo, HOA logo, lower thirds, title bars, fonts, colors) external maps such as Google or HERE! maps, still images for edit insert, voice-over, and any other required content that was not part of the flight or interior capture process should be assembled in advance if at all possible. It's extremely unfortunate when a project is held up simply because a real-estate agency didn't provide their graphic in advance.

When setting up a video project, the project will require some, if not all these listed elements. Have them on-hand in advance whenever possible.

- Agency Graphic/logo (transparency)
- HOA Graphic/logo (transparency)
- Graphic transitions (if any)

- Lower thirds/name boards (if any)
- Stock music (if any)
- Voice-over (if any)
- Title font choices (color, font, size, placements)
- Call-out graphics (virtually always needed for commercial properties)
- Agency Donuts (Open/close pieces, also referred to as "Bookends")

Some sorts of projects allow themselves to work from a stock template. In other words, the video project timeline has placeholders that simply need to be replaced with specific parts/graphics/video to fill in the project. This is by far the easiest way to work, and once a rhythm is established, save those projects as templates for time-savings in future works. Even when using a template, every project will look and feel different, because the footage, location, fonts, and graphics are different.

Building a template will help save time and generate consistency in Real Estate video production.

Leave them wanting MORE!

LENGTH OF VIDEO

Zillow, Trulia, Redfin, and other real estate sites rarely limit length of video, and of course sites for embedding such as Youtube, Vimeo, etc. do not limit video length at all. However, statistics and analytics from these sites all demonstrate that videos longer than two minutes experience severe drop-offs around the 120 second mark. If a video isn't done well, drop-offs will happen much sooner. We recommend keeping lengths to less than two minutes. If it's truly a spectacular, high value property with several unusual features, break the video down to interiors, exteriors, and unusual values (three separate videos). Allow the viewer to decide if they want to see more. There is an old saying in any sort of performance art; *"leave them wanting more."* An effective video edit will have the viewer scrambling for the phone, calling the agency looking for additional information on the property.

SETTING UP FOR THE EDIT

The typical workflow of a video is to place all relevant video on the timeline and cut away any video that isn't immediately identified as "quality." Trim the in/out point of the clips/pieces that will be kept, but don't spend too much time in this process. This is called the initial "rough-cut."

Music is then placed on the timeline and the opening shot should be lined up with the music. Typically (in real estate video), approximately three seconds are allocated for a property address and opening logo, although the opening sequence may be immediately started with interior or aerial video, perhaps with reduced opacity and address title over top. When putting the video over the music, leave enough space for the opening if there will be a logo or text-based opening.

> **Cut the music to final length FIRST to know the end point.**

Some editors prefer to edit the music to the video length first, and then place edit markers along the track for reference during the editing process. Others begin cutting video to the music, and eventually squeeze it all together. We recommend cutting music to final length first so that the end-point is always known.

MUSIC

Many real estate videos have some sort of stock music behind them. Be sure to not be using copyrighted material; it may get the editor, real estate agency, or home owner into legal troubles. There are many royalty-free music websites with downloadable audio tracks both paid and free.

> **Bed music for videos is music that is not a highlight; no dramatic shifts or heavy with lyrics.**

Choose music that offers consistency in sound. "Bed" music (music composed for video where the music is not a highlight, and rarely contains lyrics) is best used as an upbeat component of the overall presentation. Music that is devoid of dramatic shifts in sections works best. Bear in mind that as viewers are watching the video, big musical changes are likely a distraction. Find music that fits the cadence of the shooting.

For example, if the shooting cadence is fairly fast and not intended for slow-motion, be sure to use music that isn't too slow to carry the edits along. Cutting visual cues on-beat is a common means of ensuring the music carries the video message forward; most editing tools allow markers or beat indicators that will help editors cut the music to the beat.

Some tools allow the editor to break a beat down into seconds, making edits even more precise. For example, a song that is playing back at 120 beats per minute (BPM) will offer two seconds per bar, or every four beats. This is a good cadence, and the sorts of music used for real estate or corporate video generally falls in to the range of 85-130bpm, allowing cut points to be as short as 1.5 seconds per measure

> **REMEMBER: The music bed shouldn't distract and annoy, but it should organically add to the flow of the video. Background music lends itself much more to looping and reshaping than one might think. This why it is generally advised to avoid music with lyrics altogether. Search for steady rhythms and ideally some progression or development within the track which may be used for sound design.**

to 2.3 seconds per measure. Of course, video cuts are not required to fall on a measure, but it is a good practice to cut on a down beat.

Never be afraid to cut a piece of stock/bed music to better suit the video progression. For example, many pieces of bed music start smooth and simple, building into something larger. Frequently, our edits begin with the bigger piece for greatest attention, and then move to the simpler beats, building back to larger/more active segments to close out the piece. Never forget that this two-minute video needs to move quickly, keep pace, and inspire the viewer to remain eyes-on-screen. Catching viewer attention straight out of the gate by being different may be just what the viewer needed to see/hear after watching other videos.

Music to Avoid

Avoid music that has brassy instruments mixed up front, pieces that have screaming electric guitar, or obnoxious lead instruments in the front of the blend. These songs are annoying, even when quiet. One way to immediately know if a piece will work is to listen to it at a very quiet level. If nothing sticks out when it's turned down, nothing will likely stick out when it's loud, either. Avoid music that has vocals and avoid music that has any loud lead parts that suddenly stick out or jump to the front of the mix.

Other Audio Techniques

Be very cognizant of the mid-range frequencies. Many bed/ stock pieces are recorded with minimal activity in the mid-range frequencies so that voiceover can be easily inserted. However, there are many instrumental pieces that are mid-range heavy/busy, and those pieces will require a bit of audio equalization to minimize these annoying frequencies. Persons having conversations while watching the video will be easily annoyed if the midrange frequencies of their voice are drowned out or hampered due to mid-range frequencies of the background/bed music.

> **Amplify key edit points with music "Stingers"; a short sound occurring on the edit point.**

Edits may also be amplified/attention called to, via a "stinger." A stinger is a very short sound hit that usually occurs on an edit point. Finding files such as heavily reverberated big drum hits, swoosh sounds, reverse cymbals, and similar may be placed exactly on an edit point, calling attention to the next-visible edit. Stingers, also known as "One-hits," should be very subtle, to the point of nearly not being heard. They are also very effective at transition points when transitions other than crossfades are used.

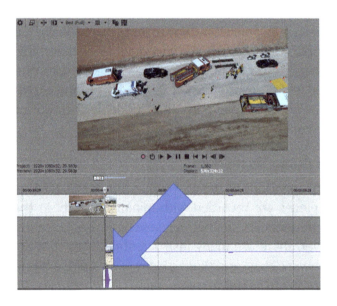

EDITING

After assembling the video on a video editing timeline, place a marker on the timeline to indicate the total length of the video. Many real estate websites will not allow video longer than two minutes in length, and with good reason. Viewers are likely looking at several homes, and the real estate agency will likely want to present as much about the property as they can, in a very short period. Plan on cutting in just enough goodness to capture attention, and no more.

Begin cutting the video, selecting only the most valuable shots, and arrange them into the scenes as requested by the agency, or in the order that the walk-through/fly overs were planned prior to the flight/walk-through. It's not necessary to be cutting/editing the video on the music beats at this point, yet experienced editors will generally begin choosing precision

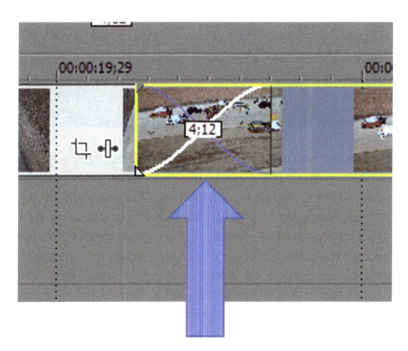

in/out points of each clip and placing the clip in-point (also known as a "head") on the music beats. Some editors allow the video clip's "tail" or out-point to trail the beat point for a half a second or so, allowing a transition between the outgoing and the incoming clip. When using transitions, the center point of the transition should align with musical beats.

Transitions

When cutting/editing video, transition points from one video event/clip to another can be either hard/jump cuts, or transitional cuts. For example, a "cross fade" from one event/clip to another 'softens' the transition (this is why the edit point tools are referred to as "transitions") may be the best method of "moving" from a UAS-to-door fly-up, transitioning to the ground-based camera that actually walks through the door and into a building or residence.

> Be sure to use transitions that fit the business model. Real estate is about selling the property. Transitions should be kept professional in nature and should align with the music and footage being used. Often, simpler is better.

Crossfades are very effective when moving from within a room to another point within the room/another view of the room and may also be used from room to room. Other types of transitions are also very effective when transiting from one room to another. Identify a transitional style that works best for the business. In our work, we typically use crossfades (xfades) for outdoor to indoor, and same-room edits. We'll use other transitional elements, such as flashes, falling blinds, or graphic/logo transitions to move into another space in the building/residence.

This sort of transition may be cute and ideal for elementary school videos; it does not belong in a professional presentation.

Avoid use of "cute" transitions; not only are they very distracting, but also shout to the world that the video was edited by an amateur. Stick with time-honored standards such as dissolves (Xfade) wipes, flashes, and pushes are all that any editor really needs. Other sorts of transitions call attention to themselves and distract from the video.

Keep transitional elements very short. Industry-standard is seven frames, or about a quarter second. Any shorter, there will be no transitional element the eye can comprehend, and much longer transitions will appear to be romantic, but slow. One of the most effective techniques that identifies the editor as an amateur is to use very long, slow crossfades. Keep the video moving by keeping transitions short.

> The average real estate video is 90 seconds to two minutes in overall length. This means the video has only 2700-3600 total frames of information to share with the viewer. Don't let a long transition take away from the limited message time available!

Titles/Transparent Graphics

Titles are a key component of any video. Colors, size, and font choice are all factors that contribute to the pacing and flow of the video. Use fonts that are contrast well with the video content underneath and choose fonts that do not have serifs.

Titles may be generated in a graphics application like Photoshop or similar, or titles may be generated inside of most video editing applications. Unless specialized titles are required, it's usually most efficient to generate titles in the video editing application, where changes on the fly are more readily available.

Sometimes, the agency, homeowner, or HOA will require graphics laid over video content, frequently in the form of a "bug" or lower third, or name board. These sorts of graphics are best sourced as transparent images in .png or .tif format so that the background has been removed from the graphic. This makes for much easier placement and image management with little or no resolution loss. Graphics for video are usually best at a resolution of 72dpi, although higher resolutions may be used (higher resolutions will slow down the final output/render process). Be sure to identify whether the agency/home owner wants an address, phone number, or email (or a combination) to close out the video. Some agencies will want a call-to-action such as "*Call today, this one won't last long!*" or similar.

This is a "bug", usually found in the lower right or upper left corner of video.

This is a lower third, usually used to present names or specific information relevant to video content. Lower thirds rarely stay on screen for longer than seven seconds.

Fine Cut

After all the graphics, titles, and general cuts are made, the edit is tweaked to its finest points. It is here that all timings, transitions, title placement, etc. are put to their final position, and the video is presentable to the client. In some cases, the video may be complete at this point, yet it's unlikely.

Color Correcting

Color correction is typically one of the last steps in the editing process, if not the last step.

Color correction may be achieved at three points in the edited timeline.

- Individual clips/events (this is used when clips are disparate and need to be better matched, not very common.
- Tracks (collection of clips on the timeline) This is a common means of correction.
- Project level (everything on all timelines) Used for bringing entire project into a particular style such as a project-wide vignette effect, or matching broadcast requirements, such as very stringent requirements by a broadcaster like PBS.

> **To streamline the color correction process, assemble similar clips on one track before beginning.**

In these sorts of projects, it's best to assemble all similar clips on one track. For example, all exterior clips captured by the UAS would be on one video track. All internal clips from inside the building on another track, all graphics on yet another track, and all titles, bugs, etc. on yet another, separate track. Using this method allows all exterior clips to be color corrected simultaneously, thus saving considerable time, and also reducing the risk of missing a clip or two when color correcting the project. The same process can be applied to interiors.

Color correction is last for multiple reasons, the first being that until all the clips are in place and have titles over them, it is difficult to know how colors from one clip to another will complement each other or mesh (outdoor to indoor is often a challenge).

Color correction typically begins with either a histogram, waveform monitor, or both.

The Vectorscope monitor allows editors to see color balance through non-judgmental eyes. A professional editor can color correct without ever seeing the picture.

Notice where colors may be leaning, towards one color or another?

Simply adjusting saturation and contrast may be enough to improve the image, and often is, assuming white balance

The left side is white-balance repaired. Small differences make a big difference.

was properly set prior to flight or indoor work. If not, many color correction toolsets offer the ability to re-set white balance by identifying a white area in the video frame.

Start any color correction process by checking white balance. If white balance appears to be correct, add saturation and contrast adjustments and work with these tools to find the right balance of color both in the waveform monitor and histogram tool. Use these tools to help understand what exactly is happening with color.

> **Color correction steps: (1) White Balance; (2) Saturation; (3) Contrast Adjustments**

If images are under or over exposed, *never* use Brightness/Contrast adjustments. Using this tool in any video editing application will raise the apparent noise in the image and will severely degrade the image quality. Use Color Curves, where brightness may be raised using the spline curves found in virtually every curving tool offered by an NLE. Using Color Curves raises the chroma value vs the luma value. In other words, the color shift will brighten any image without adding luma (light/exposure) and therefore the noise floor will not be raised.

Inserting a color wheel correction tool to the clip or track line will allow the color wheel to be used to properly correct clips. We recommend working at the track line level for most efficient and consistent result.

Color Wheel Tools

Using color-wheel correction tools offers up very powerful correction capability, as well as creative freedom to create specific scenes/styles. Color-wheel correction also opens a door to significant challenge and frustration to the uniniti- ated. However, if for example, that brown lawn needs to be green, but impact no other color or area, the Color-Wheel tools are the only efficient method of achieving specific tar- get colors/areas.

Start by moving the color wheel's center point of the mid-range wheel towards the reddish area at approximately 10 o'clock. Notice the shift in color? This will not affect very bright or very dark areas of the image. This is a tri-wheel correction and is only needed when colors are far out of accuracy.

Most video editing applications also have a single-wheel color correction tool that allows for specific color control while masking out unwanted areas.

In the following image, the grass is dull and brown due to winter. The white balance is also very cool, making the home look cold. Using the single-color wheel with a mask, the lawn is brightened, and a greener caste is given to the lawn area without affecting the colors of the home, sky, or asphalt in front of the home.

Color correction is an art, and like any art, takes time to get beyond basic proficiency. All video editors offer several tools, some of which are more common while others are more specialized. A good process to learn what each tool does is to begin with the basics and gradually move to the more advanced tools.

OTHER USES FOR sUAS

There are other real estate uses for UAS that go beyond presenting a property for sale or lease. For example, home inspectors might use the aircraft to inspect the integrity of shingles or tiles on a roof, or inspect flashing for lift, tar damage, or check gutters for damage, etc.

ROOF INSPECTIONS

It may be that any roofing company may come in and use the UAS to measure the roof for materials in the event of a replacement. EZRoof and RoofSnap are two such software applications used to determine measurements for roofing materials.

In this image, damage from lightning strikes are visible and may be demonstrated to an insurance company, homeowner, or roofing repair company.

Use of UAS allow measurements without requiring anyone to climb on ladders or walk the hips and valleys of a roofline. Roofing can be measured in/after inclement weather without fear of slipping from the roof. Some roofs are simply too steep or too high to be walked on and challenging to inspect and a UAS allows a much easier access and efficiency to inspecting these surfaces. Frequently, the hourly cost of using UAS is significantly less than the cost of insurance for someone being on the roof. Moreover, the UAS can complete the measurement in mere minutes, much faster than a human.

The primary precaution in flying roofed areas is to be aware of wind currents and rotors in roof areas. Roofs are frequently warmer, connecting with cooler air can generate currents that may be unpredictable to all but the most experienced pilot. Use caution when flying a steep roof that has multiple chimneys or other larger areas that may obstruct or deflect moving air. Stay back from these areas, use caution, and consider using a hexacopter vs a quadcopter for greater stability.

All these benefits apply to home inspectors, roofing services, general contractors, gutter installers, and anyone else who requires information prior to crawling onto the roof.

HOME INSPECTIONS

Pre-purchase home inspectors may find value in thermal cameras as well. Capturing images of a home in the early morning or late evening provides information about heat or cool air loss in a home, identifying areas where more insulation or closure of gaps is required for a more efficient home. Heat loss around windows, doors, chimney/stack areas are all immediately identified with a thermal camera.

If checking for heat loss in fall to spring seasons, the best check times are when the sun is not directly on the home. If in a warm climate, the greatest detail will be found in the cooler hours of the day, usually late afternoon or early morning.

These sorts of flights are best managed in later evening or early morning. If the thermal inspection will occur in the evening hours, a waiver to Daylight Operations, or a 107.29 waiver is required. This is in addition to the Remote Pilot Certificate requirement, and generally requires 60-90 days to obtain.

Thermal work does not require a high-resolution thermal camera, although homeowners will likely be more impressed by higher resolution images. In the world of thermal, there are three primary functions:

- **Detection** (Is there a heat source?)
- **Identification** (Is the heat source a person or a moose?)
- **Recognition** (Is the person Bob or James?)

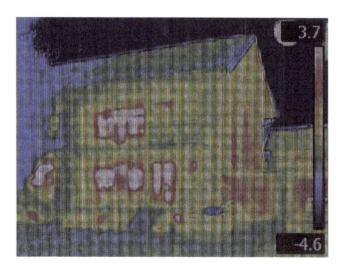

In identifying heat loss from a home or small commercial structure, a low-resolution thermal camera is all that is necessary, although there are some benefits to a higher resolution camera. Consider ROI when purchasing a thermal camera.

Pre-purchase home inspectors can use UAS to fly close to a chimney to ensure/determine if a crown is intact, or check out ridge vents, pipe boots, or other components of the roof, eaves, gutters, flashing, downspouts, and more.

Of course, all these same issues can be checked for brand new construction as well, while creating an archived record of the home at first build and may be of benefit in securing information for a home warranty.

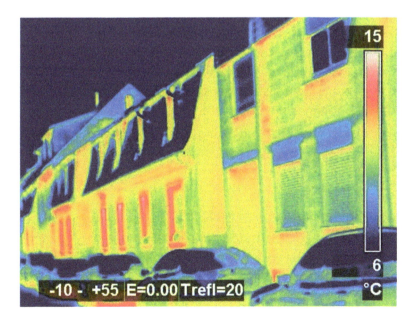

RISK MITIGATION AND SAFETY PRACTICES

> *Whoever wants to learn to fly must first learn to stand and walk and run and climb and dance: — one cannot fly into flying!*
>
> — *Friedrich Wilhelm Nietzsche*

We're all human, and we all make mistakes. Statistics demonstrate that over time, the more experience had in aviation, the more likely an error will occur. This isn't due to incompetence; in fact, errors are frequently the result of competence coupled with confidence resulting in complacency. Complacency allows us to be distracted, when confidence suggests we can expand our parametric ability due to practiced competency. Generally, this is so. However, unexpected variances can cause momentary distraction in situations where reaction to the distraction is the difference between success and failure.

> **Competence breeds confidence, yet confidence can rarely be counted as an indicator of competence.**

Introducing new risks through new experiences without proper preparation may cause us to be unconsciously incompetent. This is one of the tenets of kinesthetic learning; learn one thing and add one thing to it. Continue adding over a length of time until a broad scope of competency is developed. The broader the competency, the greater the confidence within those parameters. In other words, getting trained, understanding basics of flight, weather, environmental hazards, and unexpected situations is a critical component of becoming a qualified UAS pilot.

TRAINING

It goes without saying that risk mitigation and best practices in safety should be a component of any UAS operation.

What is chiefly needed is skill rather than machinery.
— Wilbur Wright 1900

The first step in risk mitigation is to learn to fly. Purchasing a UAS at the local big box store, watching a few YouTube videos, and zipping around the local football field does not a pilot make, although many would think otherwise. Most of the incidents logged with the NTSB to date have been the result of untrained, uneducated, unaware individuals that purchased a drone from a store, fancied themselves "skilled" because they have a lot of time playing video games, and decide they want to fly into a stadium, over a crowd, or perhaps drink and drone (that one dropped a drone on to the White House lawn!)

Worse still, those who are Part 61 manned pilots frequently bring to the table a confidence and arrogance that often has them landing UAS in trees, pounded into buildings, or CFIT (We've had several UAS students who are Part 61 pilots; they're frequently the most difficult students of all, due to knowing a lot about airplane flight and next to nothing about UAS flight).

It is highly recommended to plan on a minimum of 40 hours of flight before undertaking a simple real estate flight. Within that

> Expect to fly a minimum of 40 flight hours before undertaking a simple real estate flight. Practice launch/landings and basic maneuvers for the first 10-15 hours. Be sure to LOG your training hours too!

40 hours of training flight, the first 10-15 hours should be spent launching, landing, and learning basic maneuvers. Most organizations will not hire a pilot with less than 250 hours of practical UAS flight experience, and within that 250 hours, the pilot log-book should reflect a broad variety of unique experiences. Flying the same (or similar) flight over and over again is not "training," but rather a learned set of responses to specific stimulants.

Learn to fly for real estate by flying over a known home (the pilot's home is often a good place to start).

Any area that has an outbuilding or wide-open space to fly with a structure in the middle is a great place to begin honing skills.

Learn to fly in medium winds and learn to fly at dusk. Flying after sunset is not legal if the flight is for commercial purposes, but if there is no commercial purpose and the flight is for training or hobby purpose, there is no legal restriction for flight. More information about hobbyist flight may be found at the AMA website; https://www.modelaircraft.org/joinrenew.aspx.

> One cannot judge their own skills, it simply cannot be done - find a professional who has experience in evaluating skills.

Find a professional who has experience in evaluating skills. One cannot judge their own skills, it simply cannot be done. Going into the field and flying for money without having had third-party sign off is risky, as it's easy to get into a Dunning-Kruger situation ("*you don't know what you don't know, but are confident in your ignorance*"), and many insurance companies will not insure self-trained pilots who have no certifications for this very reason.

Although the FAA requirements for achieving a 107 test and RPC certification does not include practical evaluation doesn't mean it's a good idea. Conscientious pilots will undertake the effort to gain as much practical experience as possible.

SAFETY EQUIPMENT

In addition to safety practices, professional UAS pilots will carry equipment that helps ensure the safety of those around the flight operation, while also protecting themselves.

TRAFFIC CONES

Every UAS pilot wants to ensure that bystanders do not inadvertently walk into the area of operations, including the launch/land area, and where the pilot is controlling and viewing the UAS. Traffic cones are very inexpensive from several online or local construction supply stores. With a minimum of four, a proper operation will generally have 6-8 cones surrounding the launch/land area.

LAUNCH PAD

These pads are a matter of personal preference and each pilot will have their own ideas about whether they will or will not use a pad. Professional pilots tend to use them for several reasons. A proper launch/land pad provides a visible area where bystanders are aware of the location the UAS will be coming towards when landing. A proper launch/ land pad is large enough to keep tiny rocks and other small debris from striking props, chipping the nylon/plastic/carbon blades of the UAS, shortening their life span. The launch/land pad also helps prevent the small debris such as grass, construction debris, small rocks, dirt, or vegetation from being sucked into the motors/rotors. A proper launch/land pad also provides a flat area for the aircraft to launch/land. Finally, although not related to real estate, most launch/land pads are very bright, notifying law enforcement and emergency services where the UAS operation is being conducted.

SAFETY VEST

A safety vest should be a component of every operation. It lets bystanders know who is operating or involved in the operation of the UAS and provides high-visibility so that the pilot is not inadvertently bumped by someone not noticing the pilot. A safety vest also lends a sense of "official" to the operation.

Note every person in the operation is wearing safety vests, eyewear, and there is a launch/land pad, plus safety cones marking the operational area.

WINDMETER

A Windmeter (Anemometer) should be part of every UAS kit. Windmeters are available as stand-alone units or as smart phone-managed devices. Either work fine; we use smart-phone devices as they allow the data to be recorded and archived, providing a component of logging operations. Weatherflow manufactures them in blue or olive colors.

SANDWICH BOARD

While a sandwich board is not required, it's a great safety asset to carry. These very lightweight A-Frame boards allow the pilot and crew to notify everyone in the area that UAS operations are underway in the area, provide contact and other information, and provide an assurance that the operation is legitimate. Sandwich boards are very quick to create from any local printing supply store.

WEATHER-RELATED DECISIONS

Every professional aviator, and most casual pilots, skydivers, paraglider pilots, hang glider pilots, and anyone else whose world revolves around aviation, has a habitual interest in daily and weekly forecasts. With myriad mobile apps, Amazon Alexa, Google Home, and other technological tools surrounding our lives, it is very easy to know what is expected to come and when.

Sites like Intellicast, AviationWeather.gov, USAirnet.com, and others are all very valuable for Part 61 pilots, yet there is no system currently available that provides good ground wind or weather information. What we do know is that when a weather forecast contains a front, there will be wind. Over time and with a bit of focus, any UAS pilot becomes adept at understanding weather patterns and will be able to not only make reasonably qualified decisions in advance of weather, but also make recommendations to clients.

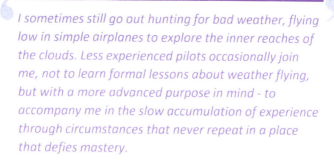

I sometimes still go out hunting for bad weather, flying low in simple airplanes to explore the inner reaches of the clouds. Less experienced pilots occasionally join me, not to learn formal lessons about weather flying, but with a more advanced purpose in mind - to accompany me in the slow accumulation of experience through circumstances that never repeat in a place that defies mastery.

— William Langewiesche 1998

Rain

It is possible to fly in light rain. With a water-treated UAS, light rain is generally not a concern. Wind frequently occurs with rain, and wind will be the greater concern. Bear in mind that any photos or video

will likely be dull and grey, and this should be explained in advance of flight, to the owner or real estate agent/agency.

When flying in rain, the other obstacle pilots will encounter is water on the lens of the camera. There are many materials available for water treating camera lenses. RainX works very well on glass lenses; do not apply RainX to plastic lenses, it may damage some plastics. Another available product is JetDry. Be sure to wipe water from the lens using a soft cloth designed for camera lenses. In the case of plastic lenses, always clear the lens of water before the moisture on the lens dries. Rain water frequently contains airborne chemicals that can permanently etch the plastic.

Flying In Wind

Environments cannot be controlled, and wind is an uncontrollable, unavoidable element of any flight environment. Flying in winds is inevitable. Having baselines for UAS flight is part of the planning process so that when winds are a point of concern, the baseline determines whether the aircraft flies or not. For example, a small quad copter is very difficult to control, and quality images will not be captured when winds exceed 11-13 mph. A larger quad system will provide slightly greater ability in high wind, but not much. High-wind systems require hex or octocopters. Set wind limits per aircraft. Put these wind limits in the organization's Policy/Procedures/Operations manuals and adhere to them. Having wind limits in writing ensures everyone knows the go/no go limits.

It's better to be on the ground wishing the aircraft was in the air, than being in the air, wishing the aircraft was on the ground.

— Aviation Cliché

We recommend that a windmeter be deployed at every operation. There are several different systems on the market. Setting up a windmeter on a tripod, everyone involved in the operation from the homeowner to the real estate agent, to the crew will recognize that standards will be observed and adhered to for safety and insurance purposes.

Wind limit recommendations

11 mph max	DJI Phantom, Autel, Yuneec Q/4K, Solo, Powervision, Walkera, most quad copters
17 mph max	Inspire 1 or Inspire 2 , GDU Byrd, S600
25 mph max	Matrice 200, Yuneec Tornado, Freefly Alta, Intuitive, Aibotix
35 mph max	Aeryon Scout, Yuneec H520, Falcon 8+

The recommended wind limits here are for open-area flight. In fact, these recommendations may be slightly lower than the manufacturer limitations; the above recommendations are based on real-world experience vs engineering specifications.

Bear in mind that open areas for real estate flight are rare; there will virtually always be streets, trees, other buildings, alleyways, and other obstacles that generate vortex'. These areas will increase wind velocity and dramatically increase the potential for rotors/unstable winds. Flying a UAS in these unstable environments is tricky at best, and a potential incident at worse. No one wants to crash the UAS into a tree, house, or driveway, even if it does miss any person, pet, or property on impact.

Reading the Wind

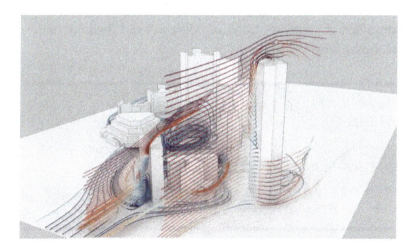

An experienced UAS pilot will know immediately that the Point of Interest/Home in this image will be a challenge if there is any wind from the North, East, or West. It will take time to learn to "read" the environment. Note the steep hill behind the home, creating one high-risk area for rotors. The long street to the west of the home creates a funnel where wind velocity will be increased. Some dissipation will occur due to trees, but with the downslope to the east, this is a very high-risk area and when low-medium winds are present, the pilot will want to exercise caution.

Wind characteristics are not only related to mechanical design and sensors; software is also significant component in wind performance, controlling the movement of the UAS on station based on input from the sensory systems, performance will vary with each system and hardware combination.

READING THE LANDSCAPE

As alluded earlier, the impact of wind over a landscape/property can be relatively easy to read. Unfortunately, the internet is full of stories and posts where pilots seem to be striking the sides of buildings, trees, or poles without the pilot understanding why.

"It was flying fine and all of a sudden it zipped up and into the side of the building."

"Everything was great until the drone had a mind of its own and flew straight to the ground."

"The drone was flying over the trees and all of a sudden it spun around and dropped into the trees."

Reading these forum conversations around the internet suggests this is a common, yet unfortunate (and avoidable) experience.

First, let's establish that flying in GPS mode may be ineffective when very close to a building. Signal may be lost, and this could explain a few of the building strikes.

I drove and hour and 15 minutes to a remote location to do an all day outdoor event yesterday. It was a good payer, so I had to do it. The winds were howling at I'm guessing 30mph with gusts to 35-38 ish. To give you an idea, there were times when I was trying to film flying sideways into the wind, and ALL the stick was planted to the right/left and I was loosing ground. I had to yaw back around, facing forward into the wind to regain my position. And even then, 16 sats would not hold position, I had to lean the right stick at 30-35% to hold. Defiantly a level 10 difficulty day. I ran 11 flights throughout different parts of the afternoon. Before you flame me for any safety issues, the only one at risk was the i1 itself. Overall, I was impressed at what this bird can take.

Expo's were set at 0.40 across the board, altitude and brake at 100%. After I got home, this tornado passed within a 1/2 mile of my house. It was quite the nerve racking day!!

However, far and away more likely in most instances the UAV was caught in a "rotor." These are also known as up/down drafts, lee waves, or cross-winds, depending on which aviation discipline one adheres to. Needless to say, these

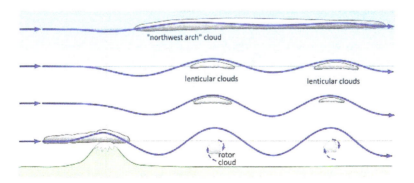

These "waves" are indicators for manned aviation and construction crews, yet the principle is only a matter of scale.

phenomena do exist, and play havoc with any sort of aerial activity whether it's wingsuiting, parasailing, skydiving, model aircraft flight, swooping, small aircraft, and particularly light-weight multirotors.

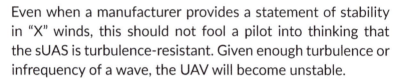

Blessed be the altitude, may it always be beneath you.
— *Douglas Spotted Eagle*

Even when a manufacturer provides a statement of stability in "X" winds, this should not fool a pilot into thinking that the sUAS is turbulence-resistant. Given enough turbulence or infrequency of a wave, the UAV will become unstable.

The first rule is to set wind limits. Small quad-craft should stay on the ground at windspeeds of greater than 12mph/5.5 meters per second. Hexacopters should consider ground-ing themselves at 22mph/10meters per second. Of course, this figure may vary depending on organizational policy and procedures manual, insurance requirements, or pay-load on the sUAS.

Being aware of wind "waves" is half the battle. Staying away from them is the rest of it. Failing the former, being able to manage the craft in turbulence is the next-best step. The GPS and accelerometer of the system will control how the aircraft responds to waves, and the pilot will want to be aware of how the UAS will react to these cycling winds.

A building blocks the wind on one side (windward side) and on the opposite side (leeward side) the wind will pay all sorts of havoc with any flying object. Winds will extend in distance up to four times the height of the obstacle, and two times the actual height.

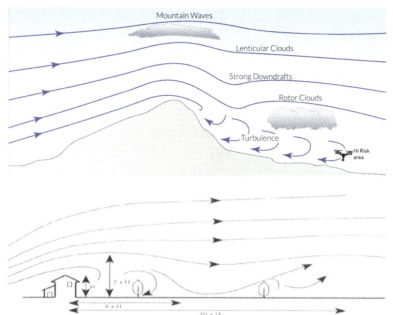

The zone of turbulence rises as the flow progresses down-stream. A building will block the prevailing wind. There is clean air above the building, and very "dirty" air next to, and the area that is **4 times the height of the building**. Avoid these areas when possible.

In terms of height, depending on wind velocity, the UAV may have to climb as high as 80' to find clean air above an obstacle. yet at 80' AGL, the winds are likely entirely different as well, depending on the weather and other obstacles in the area.

> 40×4=160 feet. Therefore, for 160' beyond the obstacle at ground level, the multirotor is at risk for catching either a down-draft or an updraft. Either way, the airframe/hull is not in clean air. In extremely high velocities (high winds) the ratio of obstacle/distance may be as great as 15X (of course, a UAS would likely not fly in these winds)!

The air goes over the obstacle and is "pulled" to the ground (downdraft), where it then "bounces" upward (updraft) and tries to resume its level flow.

These phenomena are *entirely independent* of sinks, thermal rises, dust devils, and the like.

This also occurs in natural/unbuilt up areas. Trees, canyons, ridges, rock-lines; any large object will incur rotors. Avoid them. It's virtually impossible to determine exactly where the down-draft vs. the updraft may be occurring, and the location of these dirty winds will change with wind velocity.

Flying In Urban Environments

When wind flows between buildings, the mass of the air/gas is compressed. This results in an increase in velocity. Think of squeezing hard on a tube of toothpaste, compressing the contents through the tiny hole in the end of the tube. This increases the speed/velocity at which the toothpaste squeezes out. The same thing occurs with moving air between buildings or other solid objects.

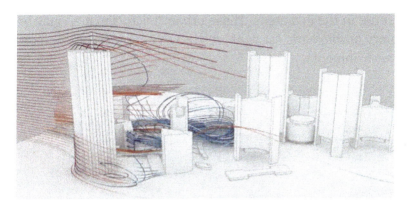

Image Courtesy of Rheologic

Depending on the wind speed, the increase may require as much as 4-10 times the distance before the winds return to "normal" velocity seen before the gap or corner.

Ground winds and winds "aloft" (*true winds aloft are beyond the reach of most UAS operations*) are rarely equal. Winds at 50′ are rarely the same as winds at ground level in an urban or suburban environment. Even small berms in the ground can cause jarring turbulence (as shown above) that

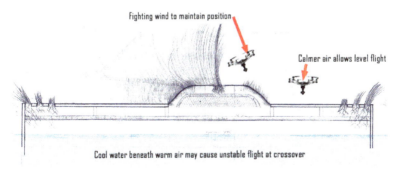

Here is a more complex example of winds blowing at 22mph in an urban environment.

settle in the low areas. These urban "microclimates" may be very problematic for light weight UAS in precision-required environments.

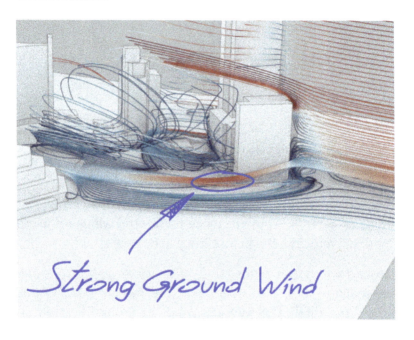

Strong Ground Wind

Compression of the flow due to building dynamics push the wind into more than 40mph in some areas. While the overall winds and reported winds in the area suggest that the wind-speed is perfectly acceptable for some commercial aircraft, turbulence and accelerated velocities within tight areas are far beyond the risk limits of most small UAS'.

Flying from warm sands to flying over water on a hot summer day may also create challenges to smooth and level flight.

In a calm sea every man is a pilot.
— John Ray

DUST DEVILS

Dust devils are summertime phenomena that can be very dangerous to humans anywhere a UAS may be flying. If they happen in a city, there is usually ample evidence of their exis-tence, as debris flies high in the "funnel." These nasty actors can show up anywhere there is hot asphalt, sand, dirt, and if that mass of rapidly moving air connects with a cool surface, they can turn violent very quickly, slinging a sUAS far from its intended flight path.

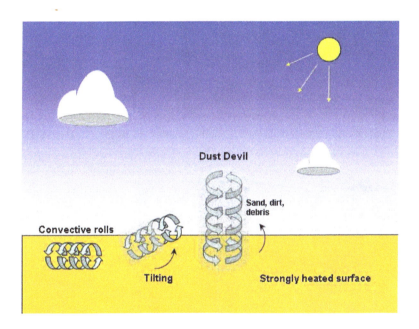

If by chance a dust devil is seen climbing in the distance, pre-pare to bring the aircraft home and land. If the dust devil is anywhere near the vehicle, climb in altitude while moving in any direction away from the dust devil. They are usually very short-lived.

Dust devils in the Nevada desert can be frightening, especially when two or three combine into one vortex.

In this softball image the dust devil is sudden, rising up in less than 3 seconds, nowhere near enough for a UAS pilot to see it build and get out of its way. IMAGE COURTESY WASHINGTON POST

How do we avoid getting caught in turbulent air? The long answer is "experience." Flying in these challenging spaces teaches us to find the lee, based on the behavior of the UAS, which will always be slightly latent to the wind.

The short answer is to study environments. Look at the wind indicators that might normally be missed. Learn to read the environment; it's not hard once one begins to look for the details around buildings, trees, brush, monuments, chimneys, and other ground obstacles. An experienced pilot will know where the challenges lie in the above home and will know when these challenges will be at their greatest point.

Two standard practices that may save pilots from troubles;

- Always use a windmeter/anemometer and check the winds frequently in midday flights.
- *Have a corporate or personal policy of a hard-deck/stop speed.* This eliminates wishy-washy/should I/shouldn't

I decisions in the field. Our cap for teaching students with a Hexacopter/Yuneec Typhoon H520 is 16mph. If a gust crosses 16, we immediately stop, and wait it out to determine the wind trendline.

- Another practice (although not standard) is to put a 5′ stream of crepe′ paper on a stick at eye level or so. This WDI, or Wind Direction Indicator, will immediately demonstrate changes in windspeed or direction, both clues that the weather may be rapidly shifting.

Crepe Paper Wind direction indicator

Determine distances from obstacles as accurately as possible prior to flight to best understand where the rotors will occur. Doing so goes a long way to maintaining control and safety when the drone is in flight. With a bit of experience, one rarely needs to worry about obstacle turbulence.

FLYING OVER WATER

Flying over water carries concern whether the flight is over open water alone, or when the flight is a mix of over water and land.

The first concern is sudden shifts in temperature from warm land to cooler water. The aircraft will either sink or rise, depending on the direction the aircraft is flying. Cool air is denser, and therefore, the aircraft will typically rise slightly when transiting land to water, and slightly sink when transiting water to land. Ensure that very low flight has buffer altitude when performing ground rush flight.

If the aircraft sensor system includes a Visual Positioning System, this should be disabled prior to flight over water. Water can create confusing returns to the VPS and may cause disorientation in the UAS.

Be aware that GPS signals can bounce on water, as can WiFi and radio.

Avoid heavy metal objects that may disorient the compass, such as boat docks, power transformer stations, phone boxes, large drainage pipes, etc.

Flight over water frequently will include winds due to the shift in temperature. Keep a watchful eye on battery levels.

> **When flying over water: keep an eye on battery levels as changes in WiFi, GPS signals, and wind shifts might affect battery efficiency.**

AWARENESS OF OBSTACLES

SITE WALKTHROUGH

Whenever possible, walk the site in advance of bidding or planning. This allows evaluation of potential hazards such as guy wires, powerlines, phone lines, columns of force/wind chasms, launch/land locations, and best time of day for best images, etc. A walkthrough also provides the opportunity to point out potential issues to agents, agencies, or property staging professionals.

Failing the ability to do a site walkthrough, the location can be previewed relatively well through Google Earth Pro (this is a free upgrade to Google Earth). However, it is common for some aerials in Google Earth Pro to be older images, and trees grow while infrastructure changes. Be advised that power or phone lines may have been installed, and trees may be larger than when the Google satellite imagery was captured.

Antennas and Power Lines

Antennas and powerlines are two of the highest-risk components of any flight. Guy wire/antenna support wires are nearly impossible to see with the best of cameras, and they do not follow a horizontal line, as they are diagonal. Antenna guy lines are important enough that the FAA has included questions about antenna guy wires in the Part 107 examination.

Power lines are a significant issue, particularly for those setting up mapping routes. Power poles vary in height, particularly at corners of property where one pole is frequently higher than others, and powerline distribution is at different heights depending on transformer placement.

Powerlines are difficult to see with a UAS reference next to them, as they are thin, frequently with no backing image enhancing the ability to determine actual vs relative height. There are several instances of mapping flights running into power lines.

No one wants to be this pilot. Ensure the flight is well away from any powerlines or guywires. It is often necessary to manually fly these locations. Consider using an observer directly below or very near guywires that are in the area.

Trees

It's not uncommon for drones to end up in trees; it seems that trees are a particular magnet for new UAS, new pilots, or perhaps both.

There are two common causes of aircraft in trees; the first being mistakes in automation (which includes low-battery or RTH/Loss of signal issues), and the second being pilots not understanding that wind changes when driving towards trees.

> **When setting up flights with automation, add 20% to the estimated height of the highest/nearest tree !**

When setting up automation programming, be entirely certain of the height of the nearest tree and add a 20% safety buffer. If flying inside a tree-cut area that is ringed by trees, either plan the flight cleanly by walking the area to input automation points or ensure that very highly accurate and detailed maps are available.

The same applies to setting up Auto Return/Return to Home, etc. Prior to flight, take the time to open the menu/settings for the UAS and set the RTH altitude 15-20% higher than the tallest obstacle in order to avoid the UAS striking an object while returning home due to low battery or loss of contact with the GSC.

A tree is a big obstacle and absorber of wind. When flying in a headwind towards a tree, the closer to the tree the UAS becomes, the more likely it is to be "sucked in" due to the lower turbulence and the pilot driving hard against a headwind. When the headwind is suddenly gone due to the windbreak of the tree's leaves/branches, the UAS surges forward and strikes the tree. The same can happen when flying towards features on a building that may be blocking or routing wind. Use caution when winds are higher than 4-5 mph. As previously recommended, always use a windmeter and check its output any time a small shift in windspeed or direction are noted.

Visual Observers

A Visual Observer is a partner to the pilot, also known as a "V/O." The V/O is responsible for eyes on UAS at all times. The V/O also may be valuable when neighbors come to the operations area asking questions about the UAS and what activity is taking place (this is a common occurrence in residential real estate).

V/O's are not required unless the pilot is using First Person Video goggles/glasses. In the event the pilot is wearing a goggle or other device which prevents unaided view of the aircraft, a V/O is required by the Federal Aviation Regulations (FARs).

The Remote Pilot in Command (PIC) is responsible for training/instructing the Visual Observer.

The V/O is more than just a friend who "tags along." The V/O should be fully trained in looking out for other aircraft, proximity to obstacles, persons near the operational area, and any potential distractions. The V/O should be trained to calmly and clearly communicate issues, vs excitedly yelling "*There's a helicopter coming right at you, GET DOWN, GET DOWN!*"

Ideally, the V/O is located next to the pilot, or near the pilot, yet not in a position to crowd the pilot. In some situations, our crew employs hands-free radio systems for the V/O, pilot, and other involved parties, enabling the pilot and V/O to communicate while keeping the entire crew informed. This sort of system requires radio training and discipline to ensure the pilot is not distracted by external chatter.

PREFLIGHT

Pre-flighting the UAS is a requirement of the Federal Aviation Regulations (FARs). To not preflight any aircraft and area is simply stupid and unnecessarily increases risk to person, property, and aircraft.

PREFLIGHT THE UAS CREW

Preflight Person (Pilot self-check) Aviation has several risk-management safety mnemonics. They can be instituted to UAS flight operations as well. Two of our favorite mnemonics;

"IM SAFE"

- Illness: Am I suffering from any illness or symptom of an illness which might affect me in flight?
- Medication - Have I taken any drugs (prescription or over-the-counter)?
- Stress - Am I overly worried about other factors in my life? The psychological pressures of everyday living can be a powerful distraction and consequently affect a pilot's performance.
- Alcohol - Has at least eight hours passed since my last alcoholic drink?
- Fatigue - Have I had sufficient sleep and adequate nutrition?
- Emotion - Am I angry, bothered by a challenging conversation, thinking about the driver that cut me off on the way to this job?

"PAVE"

Another mnemonic

- **P**ilot
- **A**ircraft
- en**V**ironment
- **E**xternal factors

PreFlight the UAS

Preflight the UAS. Have a preflight checklist for every component of the operation. Camera, motors, props, aircraft control surfaces, remote, displays, any additional radio systems, etc. See the Appendix in this book for a pre-flight checklist.

Pre-flight/pre-launch mnemonic for UAS:

"**Lights** (powered up), **Camera** (sensors powered/sending), **Action!**" (props at launch/lift speed)

And one more mnemonic:

CIGAR

- **C**ontrols check (no skips, catches, full movement of all control components on the Ground Station Control)
- **I**nstruments check (all sensors properly reading such as Sonar, camera, GPS)
- **G**as/fuel (Battery level is acceptable for flight)
- **A**ttitude (propellers in good condition, no chips, dents, and properly angled)
- **R**unup (check up/down/yaw/forward/backward/side movement prior to beginning mission)

> **UAS calibration should occur when the UAS has travelled further than 50 miles from its last calibration point.**

Recall where the last calibration occurred. Manufacturers have different recommendations, but it's a good idea to recalibrate any time the UAS has traveled further than +/50 miles from the last calibration point. Some organizational PPO's require each UAS to be recalibrated prior to every flight. Some organizational PPO manuals require logging of each calibration. Consult with the insurance agency's policy/operations manual (if there is one).

PreFlight the Area to be Flown

This is particularly important if the area wasn't previously walked prior to the bidding process, but should occur in any circumstance, no matter how well the property may be known.

Preflight the Control Area

Ensure there is plenty of space to move about, clean visual lines of sight to the flight area, no obstacles to block radio communication, and free of hazards. Identify areas where pets, people, or personnel might be a problem.

> **Identify the emergency landing areas.**

Identify alternate landing areas, also known as an "out," used in the event of a sudden need to bring the UAS to the ground. Always plan on fail-safes. Have plans in the event environmental issues shorten the flight through reduced battery life, if a prop is damaged, if a motor should seize, or any other issue requires an immediate landing.

Set the RTH altitude. Contrary to popular believe, RTH should vary from location to location.

Depending on the area, waiver requirements, or organizational policy, set any geofence parameters.

> Geofencing enables flight planners to ensure that the UAS will not go outside of horizontal (and in some cases, vertical) boundaries. Geofencing may be valuable in assuring neighbors that the aircraft will not fly over their homes, or that fly-aways are limited by the geo-fence parameters.

Post-Flight

Although post-flight practices may not initially be considered a component of risk management, this step helps identify the challenges that may have occurred in the flight operation. Examining the operation post-flight offers up the opportunity for the crew (or single pilot) to self-examine, asking the question of "what went well, what didn't go so well, and if given another opportunity for this flight, what would/should be different? Post flight debriefs should be respectful, yet brutally honest. Even if the pilot is a solo operator, the post mortem conversation should take place. Additional post flight actions include:

- Turn the power off to the UAS and/or disconnect the batteries.
- Power down the transmitter.
- Power down any external photo/video equipment.
- Check pictures: Verify that the UAV camera actually took the pictures.
- Visually check UAS for signs of damage and/or unusual wear.
- Secure the aircraft.

Post-Flight Briefings:

1. What went well?
2. What would you change to make it better /easier next time?

- Log flight.
  - ○ Logging the flight frequently is the motivator for the post-flight debrief, and information gleaned during the debrief should be archived in the logbook.

While all these various applications of safety practices may seem overly cautious, over time the value of a conservative approach will reveal itself. The pilot to be trusted isn't the pilot that has "never crashed." The pilot to be trusted has had multiple minor (or a major) mishap, has learned from them, and not repeated the experience. Agencies should be wary of any pilot that boasts of *"never crashing,"* or who says *"I've never even broken a prop"* before. These sorts of statements should be red flags indicating a lack of experience, and warrant a second look at the pilot's portfolio, time in industry, and level of activity.

He is most free from danger, who, even when safe, is on his guard.
— Publilius Syrus

Glossary of Drone Terminology[1,2]

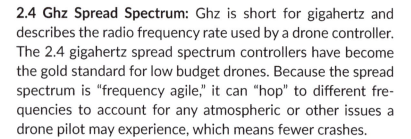

Technology is a useful servant but a dangerous master.
— Christian Lous Lange

2.4 Ghz Spread Spectrum: Ghz is short for gigahertz and describes the radio frequency rate used by a drone controller. The 2.4 gigahertz spread spectrum controllers have become the gold standard for low budget drones. Because the spread spectrum is "frequency agile," it can "hop" to different frequencies to account for any atmospheric or other issues a drone pilot may experience, which means fewer crashes.

5.8GHz: Used in hobby and professional grade RC drones. A live feed sent from a drone's camera that provides better range and less lag, very popular in FPV racing and usually paired with a set of FPV Goggles.

808 Camera: This is a common term for a range of very small cameras, which are often sold as keychain cameras. They are extremely lightweight and are used by hobbyists to take pictures from a multi-rotor aircraft.

250 Racer: Term to describe a racing multicopter that's 250mm diagonally from end to end. Very common type of quadcopter currently among FPV racers.

A

Accelerometer: A device that measures the acceleration forces in a certain direction and helpful in maintaining the Drones orientation. These devices are used to stabilize quadcopters.

Acro: Short for Acrobatic Mode. Best for doing freestyle tricks and for precise flight control.

Aerial Photography: the hobby of capturing images and video while in the air with a camera mounted to your drone.

AGL: Altitude above ground level.

Altitude Hold function: Allows pilot to focus on the camera while the drone hovers steadily in air by itself at a set height. An onboard barometer is needed to allow Altitude Hold.

ARF: Almost ready to fly. ARF units will many times come without the transmitter and may require some assembly.

Autopilot: A capability of a drone to conduct a flight without real-time human control. For example, following pre-set GPS coordinates.

Autonomous Flight: There are some UAVs that are managed by internal programming that have instructions on where to fly as guided by an onboard GPS system. This is in opposition to steering mechanisms that are operated by radio control from the ground.

Axis: One plane of potential flight. Most quadcopters have at least 4 axis controls, with 6+ being preferred.

B

Balanced Battery Charger: This is a charger or an internal system for Lipo batteries (or different chemistries) which uses smart technology to charge multiple cells properly that are located within the battery and balances them.

Barometric Pressure Sensor: This device used barometric readings to determine the altitude of the aircraft. It can help drones to be able to calculate their height above the ground, along with using combinations of other sensors. (Enables Altitude Hold feature)

Battery – Various batteries are used on drones. The onboard battery may power the flight controller, the receiver, the FPV transmitter, and the rotors (via ESC's)

Betaflight: Flight controller configuration software.

Bind: This is the process of making the controller (Transmitter) communicate with the drone.

BNF: Bind N Fly. The unit is ready to bind to your transmitter and fly.

Brushless Motor: These motors have permanent magnets that rotate around a fixed armature, which eliminates any problems that could be associated with connecting current regarding a moving part. The brushless motors are much more efficient and hardy than brushed motors.

Build: A unit that is built at home as opposed to one that is store bought.

BVLOS: Beyond visual line of sight.

C

Camera gimbal: This is the holder of the camera used on drones. It can tilt and swerve, thanks to the servos that power it. The gimbal is strong enough to support even large DSLR cameras.

CF: Short for Carbon Fiber, the composite material used to build most racing quadcopters. Known for its strength and durability.

Channel – This can refer to the frequency an FPV transmitter is using (for video from a drone), or an assigned function linking a controller transmitter with a drone. For instance, a channel may be assigned to control throttle, or turning lights on and off. Most drones use at least 6 channels for control.

Cleanflight: Flight controller configuration software.

CFIT (See-fit) Controlled Flight Into Terrain. This is a kind way of saying someone crashed due to human error.

Collision Avoidance Many UAVs have collision avoidance systems to prevent pilots from flying into fixed objects or other aircraft. It is also known as sense and avoid.

Commercial Flight: flying a drone for money-making purposes. This is currently restricted by FAA regulations unless you have a **Remote Pilot Certificate with a Small Unmanned Aircraft Rating.**

Controller (sometimes 'Flight controller'): A handheld device that is used by the drone pilot to control the drone. Controllers are also called a transmitter or radio. The computer on the drone that helps the drone fly. Controllers can be as simple as taking radio signals and signaling the ESC's, to working with accelerometers, GPS, and other sensors to control all aspects of the drone's flight

D

Drone: also known as unmanned aerial vehicles (UAVS), are aircraft without a human pilot aboard. They are either controlled by pilots on-the-ground, or autonomously via a pre-programmed mission.

E

(ESC) Electronic Speed Control: The device for controlling an electric aircraft's motor. It is the connection between the RC receiver and main battery. It usually includes a Battery

Elimination Circuit (BEC), which provides the power for the onboard electronics like an autopilot and the RC system.

F

FAA: Federal Aviation Administration A United States Department of Transportation Agency, with the authority to regulate and oversee all aspects of American civil aviation.

Fail Safe: System that helps protect a multicopter in case of some type of error. For example, if a quadcopter loses control signal, a failsafe will have the quadcopter return to the point of takeoff (return home).

FAR: Federal Aviation Regulation

FC (Flight Controller) is the brain of the multirotor.

First Person View: Also known as FPV, a system in which the drone operator views the camera footage from the drone in real-time. The video stream is either viewed through a pair of special goggles, or to a device like a tablet or smartphone.

Firmware: Software loaded into the microprocessor-based products' non-volatile memory. The reason it is referred to as firmware is because it remains in non-volatile memory state even when power is removed. In the autopilots case, it is an application (App for smart phone users) or program that determines how and what the auto pilot does.

Flight Control System: This is a network of controls that is interconnected and allows the pilot to fly the quadcopter or any other multi-rotor airborne vehicle.

Fly Away: Unintended flight outside of operational boundaries (altitude/airspeed/lateral) as the result of a failure of the control element or onboard systems, or both.

Fly-Away Protection System: A system that will return the UAV safely to the surface, or keep it within the intended operational area, when the link between the pilot and the UAV is lost.

FOV (Field of View) FOV refers to the measurement of how much environment you can see through a camera lens, usually measured in degrees.

FPV: Acronym for "First Person View." This is also known as "Remote Person View" (RPV). FPV is from a camera (such as GoPro) mounted on the front or bottom of the Quadcopter which allows the operator to view exactly what the aerial vehicle is viewing in real time.

FPV camera: A special camera used for first-person-view racing, piloting, photography, or videography.

FPV goggles: A special set of goggles used to view what the multirotor's camera is seeing in real time.

FPV Racing: A sport in which pilots race small quadcopters around a predetermined track.

Frequency: The radio frequency FPV equipment runs on. Can be brand-dependent. Allows for multiple channels so pilots don't interfere with each other.

FSIM: Flight Standards Information Manual. Somewhat more important than the FAR, this advises ASI's how to interpret the FAR.

G

Geofencing: The use of GPS technology to create a virtual geographic boundary, enabling software to trigger a response when a drone enters or flies within a particular area.

Gimbal: This is a specialized mount for a camera, giving it the ability to swerve and tilt by utilizing servos. This gives the camera the capability of staying in one position, regardless of the movement of the drone. This allows for a very smooth and stabilized looking image.

GIS: Geographic Information System designed to capture, store, manipulate, analyze, manage, and present spatial or geographic data.

GPS: Global Positioning System that is used to track the position of an object in relation to the global spatial plane, track movement, or cause an airborne vehicle such as a quadcopter to hold position.

Ground Control Station: GSC. This software runs on the ground on a computer. It receives telemetry information via an airborne UAV. It displays its status and progress. This frequently includes sensor and video data. It can also be used for transmitting in-flight commands up to the UAV in the air.

Gyroscope: A gyroscope or gyro, measures the rate of rotation of the UAV and helps keep the craft balanced correctly with respect to yaw, pitch and roll. Helps to maintain the orientation of the quadcopter while in flight. In most cases, quadcopters use a triple-axis gyroscope.

H

Head tracking: A feature on some goggles that allows you to maneuver your camera's angle during flight by moving your head up and down or side to side.

Headless Mode: (see IOC) regardless of the orientation of the craft or the way the front of the craft is pointed, it will follow your stick movements.

Hexacopter: A multi-rotor aircraft having six rotors in which the beauty and advantage of the hexacopter is that it can lose any single engine and still maintain control to land.

Hobbyists are noncommercial pilots that fly UAVs domestically. Their aircrafts can't go more than 400 feet in altitude and must be line-of-sight.

I

IMU: The Inertial Measurement Unit is a controller which combines an accelerometer and a gyro, with the purpose of helping with the orientation and stabilization of a quad.

INS – Inertial Navigation System: This is a means of calculating position that is based on the initial GPS reading. This is followed by speed and motion sensor readings that use dead reckoning. This is useful when the GPS has lost its signal temporarily or is not available.

IOC: Intelligent Orientation Control – Usually, the forward direction of a flying multi-rotor is the same as the nose direction. By using Intelligent Orientation Control (IOC), wherever the nose points, the forward direction has nothing to do with nose direction.

J

Jello: Undesired effect of vibration impacting video. Video appears distorted like jello jiggling, caused by the multirotor itself. Can be corrected with use of a quality Gimbal camera mounting device.

L

LAANC system: Low Altitude Authorization and Notification Capability system, an industry developed application with the goal of providing drone operators near real time processing of airspace notifications and automatic approval of requests for flights that are in controlled airspace.

Landing Gear comes in various sizes (tall/short), and is the undercarriage of an aircraft, including the wheels or pontoons on which it rests while not in the air.

LCD monitor: A screen, usually attached to the controller, used to view what a multirotor's camera is seeing. Usually used instead of goggles.

LiPo: Short for Lithium Polymer, LiPo is the type of battery favored by most drone manufacturers due to its low weight and maximized charge capacity and power. Although LiPos are safe, be aware overcharging the battery or breaking the flexible polymer case could result in fire.

Lithium Polymer battery: LiPo or LiPoly. The Lithium Ion battery (Li Ion) is a variant. Lighter weight and more power is offered by this battery chemistry compared to NiCad and NiMh batteries.

LOS: Short for **Line of Sight,** refers to being able to see your drone from your operating position with your naked eye. Your drone should always be within your line of sight.

M

mAh: milli Amp Hours. A unit of measurement that describes how much 'power' a battery can provide before it needs to be recharged.

Mod: modifications Drone addicts do to their machines to integrate new functions or cool features. These changes are usually called mods.

Mode 1 transmitters: have throttle on the right stick and are popular in the UK.

Mode 2 transmitters: have throttle on the left stick and are more popular in the USA.

Multicopter: A generic name for a drone with multiple propellers, also known as rotors. Depending on the number of rotors, there are tricopters, quadcopters, hexacopters, octocopters and so on.

Multi-rotor copters: are referred to by many names, which include: Drone, Quadcopter, Quadricopter or Quadrocopter.

N

Nano: an extremely small drone, can fit in the palm of your hand and easy to fly indoors.

NAS (National Airspace System): is the airspace, navigation facilities and airports of the United States along with their associated information, services, rules, regulations, policies, procedures, personnel and equipment. It includes components shared jointly with the military.

NAZA: is a flight controller that is used on the DJI Phantom Drones and it contains the main control chip, an accelerometer, a gyroscope and a barometric altimeter.

No Fly Zone: Areas where flying a drone is restricted by government regulations. Areas where a drone could interfere with an airplane or record sensitive information make up most of these areas.

O

Octocopter: A drone with 8 horizontal propellers or rotors.

OSD: Abbreviation for "On Screen Display" which shows flight data in text or graphical form. Typically used to show telemetry information such as speed, battery life, heading, etc.

P

Part 107: Required in the US when operating a drone for commercial purposes. Refers to CFR Part 107 of the Federal Aviation Regulations for non-hobbyist unmanned aircraft operations, which covers a broad spectrum of commercial uses for drones weighing less than 55 pounds.

Payload: The amount of additional weight a drone is able to lift in addition to its own weight and batteries. If you attach a camera and gimbal to your drone, the combined weight is the payload.

PDB: Stands for Power Distribution Board. Component which allows the power from the battery to be distributed to all the various components on a craft.

PIC (Pilot in Command): This is the person who is ultimately responsible for the operation and safety during flight of an unmanned aerial vehicle.

Pitch: A measure which describes the flight angle along one axis, usually measured from level in case of aerial vehicles. Forward and Backwards motion.

Pre-Flight Planning: The activities conducted by the pilot and flight crew prior to takeoff to ensure that the flight will be conducted safely and in accordance with all applicable standards and regulations. The activity includes, but is not limited to, such things as checking weather, route of flight, airspace, equipment configuration, support personnel, terrain and communications requirements.

Power Distribution Board: is the PDB and is a board that is used on the multicopters to help distribute the power to each of the motors to provide proper stabilization of the unit.

Prop: Short for Propeller.

Q

Quadcopter: or **Quad** that typically has 4 propellers, each with its own motor and propeller, situated in a square forma-tion for smooth and precise flight.

R

Raceband: A set of 5.8ghz frequencies commonly used in Drone racing when multiple pilots are flying.

Radio: also known as a transmitter or Controller, set to broad-cast on a specific frequency or channel that sends a signal to control pitch, yaw, roll direction of the drone.

Radio Controller: wireless handheld device used to control flight of the drone.

R/C : Synonym for Radio Controlled.

RC: Shorter way of writing "Radio Controlled – it refers to control of a drone via radio waves.

Receiver: Accepts the camera's feed and relays it to your screen/goggles of choice.

Return to Home: A GPS feature that returns the drone to the "home" position where it took off.

RTF: Ready to Fly – This means the drone is sold with every-thing needed in the pack. All you need to do is charge the bat-teries and you are ready to use it. It is possible you may need to buy the batteries separately for the controller. This fact is usually mentioned on the box.

Rx: Abbreviation for Receiver.

S

Sense and Avoid: The capability of a UAS to remain well clear from and avoid collisions with other airborne traffic. Sense and Avoid provides the functions of self-separation and collision avoidance.

Servo: A shorter name for servomotor or servomechanism. Aerial vehicles use servomotors for various functions such as pan cameras and wing flaps adjustments which can be controlled from the ground.

Spotter: a person that keeps track of your drone by line-of-sight while you fly via FPV. They can let you know about hazards which may be out of your field of view through the goggles.

sUAS: is short for – **s**mall **U**nmanned **A**ircraft **S**ystem.

T

Telemetry – Data referring to all aspects of a flying drone. Speed, altitude, pitch, roll, yaw, battery life, position, etc.

Throttle: Control that influences the RPM or the speed of electric motors. Higher throttle generates more thrust.

Thrust: The combined amount of force from a propeller and a motor which generates lift. Lift is what takes you up and into the sky.

Transmitter: A device that sends commands to the drone from the pilot or a component that relays the camera's feed to the receiver located on the goggles.

Trim: Setting to adjust the way a drone hovers. Adjusting trim settings can help to keep it in place while hovering.

TX: Abbreviation for transmitter or transmit.

U

UAV: unmanned aerial vehicle. A device that can propel itself through the air without a pilot onboard. Drones and quadcopters are UAVs.

Ultrasonic sensor: A sensor that uses the ultra sound wavelength to communicate with a transmitter. In aerial vehicles, ultrasonic sensors are used for calculating the distance to the ground by bouncing sound waves back and forth. They don't work further than a few meters from the ground.

UTM: Abbreviation for Unmanned Traffic Management, a concept created by NASA to safely integrate manned and unmanned aircraft into low altitude airspace. This cloud-based system will help manage traffic at low altitudes and avoid collisions of UASs being operated beyond visual line of sight.

V

Video Latency: Lag in what your camera sees and when it transmits it to your monitor or goggles.

Visual line of sight: is the term that is going to control how the pilot can see the aircraft from the ground without the use of artificial vision.

Visual Observer: A crew member who assists the UAS pilot in the duties associated with collision avoidance. This includes, but is not limited to, avoidance of other traffic, airborne objects, clouds, obstructions, and terrain. Most associated with FPV flying.

VLOS: Abbreviation for Visual Line of Sight.

VRX: video receiver.

VTX: Abbreviation for video transmitter, connected to your camera and transmits the video signal from your drone back to you down on the ground in real time.

W

Waiver - The FAA issues waivers (or authorizations) to certain requirements of Part 107 if an applicant demonstrates they can fly safely under the waiver without endangering people or property on the ground or in the air.

Waypoint: A set of coordinates which define a point in space. Waypoints are useful in designing various autonomous missions for quadcopters. Mapping out would be impossible without a possibility to define these physical locations.

WiFi FPV: Mostly found on cheaper drones, usually performed by a downloaded APP. which you connect to in order to fetch the live feed. The signal is compatible with most Android/iOS smartphones and tablets.

WOT (Wide Open Throttle) – When the throttle stick on a controller is pushed all the way forward.

Y

YAW: The describes the quadcopter rotation around it's center axis on a level plane.

---

[1] Airdronecraze.com. 2017. "Quick Reference Guide Of Drone Terminology." Retrieved Feb. 28, 2018 (https://www.airdronecraze.com/quick-reference-guide-of-drone-terminology/).

[2] Go Professional Cases. 2017. "UAV, Drone And Multirotor Glossary Of Terms." Retrieved Feb. 28, 2018 (https://goprofessionalcases.com/drone-case-resources/uav-and-drone-and-multirotor-glossary-of-terms).

SUNDANCE MEDIA GROUP

ABOUT SUNDANCE MEDIA GROUP

Based in Las Vegas, Nevada and West Jordan, Utah, Sundance Media Group (SMG), have been producing training for trade events, public safety organizations, and private individuals for more than 20 years. Instructors from SMG have taught, presented workshops and have participated in panels worldwide. Over the years, SMG's area of focus has been audio, video and software applications for production and post-production. Douglas Spotted Eagle, the original founder of SMG, has long history of aviation, from the adrenaline-filled world of fast-action videography in skydiving to commercial application of drone/UAV use. SMG's latest evolution and vision is to incorporate its years of experience for best-practices training into the world of UAV use.

SMG serves as a consultant within the UAV industry, offering training and speaking engagements on UAV topics ranging from, but not limited to: UAV cinematography, commercial and infrastructural UAV applications, UAV risk management, night UAV flight, aerial security systems, and 107 training to ensure pilots clearly understand the FAA laws. SMG has intimate knowledge of the FAA FARs and FSIM; our collective experience with instructors and UAV pilots nationwide is our foundation for creating a best-practices for everything drone/UAV/UAS. The greatest strengths in the SMG lineup of consulting and education services are the vertical-specific training programs for Public Safety, Construction, Vertical Inspections, Journalists, Cinematographers, Thermal uses, and mapping/infrastructure development.

JENNIFER PIDGEN

As the majority owner and COO of Sundance Media Group (SMG), Jennifer is dedicated to developing the sUAS/UAV training programs and strategic industry partnerships. A marketing guru with over 20 years of marketing experience within the consumer electronics and photo/video channels, Jennifer manages large-scale training events and vendor/sponsor relationships. No stranger to logistical and analytical reporting, Jennifer manages all sUAS/UAV logistics and overall SMG operations, including applying for SMG's ISO certification. Bearing a degree in finance/accounting, Jennifer also holds a USPA regional wingsuit and speed skydiving judge rating. Jennifer's diverse background in science, math, and marketing are a remarkable combination within the sUAS industry as her education, experience, entrepreneurship, and passions are put to good work. Ultimately, her expertise is inspiring conversation and cultivating mutually-beneficial partnerships; each with a focus towards building a successful and safe sUAS/UAV community.

Douglas Spotted Eagle

Douglas Spotted Eagle is a giant in the video and audio production industries, having received Grammy, Emmy, DuPont, Peabody, and many other awards. Douglas is the original founder and primary instructor and industry consultant for Sundance Media Group, Inc. and VASST, authoring several books and DVDs and serving as an advisor and guide for videographers, software manufacturers and broadcasters. Douglas is a well-known musician and a world-travelled speaker/instructor. Since 2005, Douglas has focused his energy and experience within the UAV/sUAS industry and aerial photography as a skydiver and pilot.

Skydiving since 2006 and instructing UAS since 2012, Douglas is an accomplished aerial photographer who thrives in the adrenaline-filled world of fast-action videography. Appointed as a Safety and Training Advisor in the aviation world, he is a risk management/mitigation subject matter expert and has received multiple Chesley H. Judy safety awards. Douglas also brings intimate knowledge of the FAA FARs and FSIMs. Douglas' vision is to incorporate his years of imaging and aviation experience into best-practices for everything drone/UAV/UAS. Douglas is a frequent (and dynamic!) speaker and consults on many UAS subjects.

Meet our other instructors on our website:
www.sundancemediagroup.com

SPECIAL THANKS TO:

Dave Fahrny & Suzie Marquardt for the photos graciously lent to this book, James Spear, who is always there to lend a good word and a strong hand, Jack Spear, for reading all our books before they go to publication, Dave Morris, for helping us bring these books to life, our parents for giving us the motivation to write, Emerald Exhibitions for providing us a platform, Interdrone and staff for their tremendous support, manufacturers such as DJI, Intel, Autel, GDU, Yuneec, Hoodman, FoxFury, Venom Power, for providing the tools we use to create and instruct.

Kevin J, Paul H, thanks for lending your inspirations and one of your homes to this book.

We're also grateful to the software manufacturers that have supported us in our endeavors, both practical and theoretical, with a specific nod to the Pix4D, Dronify, and DroneDeploy teams.